Verses From Essex
Edited by Annabel Cook

First published in Great Britain in 2008 by:
Young Writers
Remus House
Coltsfoot Drive
Peterborough
PE2 9JX
Telephone: 01733 890066
Website: www.youngwriters.co.uk

All Rights Reserved

© Copyright Contributors 2007

SB ISBN 978-1 84431 405 8

Foreword

Young Writers was established in 1991 and has been passionately devoted to the promotion of reading and writing in children and young adults ever since. The quest continues today. Young Writers remains as committed to the nurturing of poetic and literary talent as ever.

This year's Young Writers competition has proven as vibrant and dynamic as ever and we are delighted to present a showcase of the best poetry from across the UK and in some cases overseas. Each poem has been selected from a wealth of *Little Laureates* entries before ultimately being published in this, our sixteenth primary school poetry series.

Once again, we have been supremely impressed by the overall quality of the entries we have received. The imagination, energy and creativity which has gone into each young writer's entry made choosing the poems a challenging and often difficult but ultimately hugely rewarding task - the general high standard of the work submitted ensured this opportunity to bring their poetry to a larger appreciative audience.

We sincerely hope you are pleased with this final collection and that you will enjoy *Little Laureates Verses From Essex* for many years to come.

Contents

Blenheim County Primary School

Jade Oliver (8)	1
Kieran Halls (8)	1
Abigail Last (9)	1
Ellie Kavanagh (9)	2
Chloe Williams (9)	2
Mollie Chalkley (8)	2
Louis Chitticks (9)	3
Jarrod Mullett (9)	3
Niamh Finnegan (8)	3
Amy Eden (9)	4
Storm Booth (9)	4
Charlie Waterman-Walden (9)	4
Joe Emberson (8)	5
Connor Andrews (9)	5
Ellis Misirlisoy (8)	5
Elspeth Macnab-Stark (9)	6
Laura Moore (8)	6
Sonny Lock (8)	7
Karis Nash (8)	7
Sophie Phillips (8)	7
Rebecca Nolan (8)	8
Charley Price (8)	8
Leticia Rigg (8)	8
Connor Stephens (8)	9
Krysten Tobin (8)	9
Jack Andrews (9)	9
Owen Treais (8)	10
Emily Allen (8)	10
Danielle Burgess (8)	10
Alfie Cook (8)	11
Faith Gensberg (8)	11
Jason Harrold (8)	11
Kacey Holloway (8)	12
Keith Hoang (8)	12
Nicholas Harris (8)	12
Lucy Johns (8)	13

Hacton Primary School

Adam Trinder (10)	13
Jake Harris (10)	14
Ben Hatton (10)	14
Chloe Fordham (10)	15
Gareth Pownall (10)	15
Cassie Finch (10)	16
Sophia Harris (10)	17
Taylor Kearney (10)	18
Chloe White (10)	18
Daniel Coombs (10)	19
Danny Wallace (10)	19
Shannon Morton (10)	20
Jay Cappleman (10)	20
Sally Cleary (11)	21
Louise Crockford (10)	21
Amy Miller (10)	22
Amber Cundall (10)	22
Daniel Powell (10)	23
Shars Jerke (10)	24
Jimmy Marriner (10)	24
Bobby James (11)	25
Grace Redwood (10)	25
Emma Roberts (10)	26
Megan Wilson-Storey (11)	26
Rebecca Howell (9)	27
Abbie Gay (10)	27
Renée Dacres (10)	28
Aaron Bolton (9)	28
Jessica Lovell (10)	29
Aran Güner (10)	30
Sean Faulkner (10)	30
Sam Jeffs (10)	31
Molly Sparks (11)	31
Mustafa Khraishi (11)	32
Luke Bolton (11)	32
Aycin Kaya (9)	33
Alex Wheeler (10)	33
Laura Wood (9)	34
Joseph Triggs (9)	34
Charlie Howsego (9)	34

Devon Perkins (10)	35
Peter Martin (10)	35
Rylan Purnell (10)	35
Elisha Seymour (9)	36
Caitlin Dible (9)	36
Edward Vulpe (9)	37
Alex Secular (9)	37
Alex Cordaro (9)	38
Dean Wedge (9)	38
Lewis Bennett (9)	39

John Perry Primary School

Taylor Smith (7)	39
Ellie Patience (8)	40
Joshua Ratford (7)	40
Bethany Livesey (7)	41
Cheyenne Borg (7)	41
Brooke Shore (7)	42
Chloe Moore (7)	42
Jessica-Anne Manning (7)	42
Emily Brett (7)	43
Harry Addison (7)	43
Joe Sullivan Sparks (7)	43
Mollie Wilson (7)	44
Matthew Ramsden (7)	44
Abbie Maulkerson (7)	45
Joy A Utonwanne (7)	45
Kane Hearn	46
Macey Rees	46
Shelby Pickering (7)	46
Tegan Churchill (7)	47

Katherine Semar Junior School

Reece Jackson (8)	47
Craig Carey (9)	47
Jessica Jozunas (8)	48
Jade Hunt (8)	48
Nathan Richardson (8)	48
Almas Ahmed (8)	49
Conor McCabe (8)	49
Bryony Wright (8)	49

Name	Score
Callum Courtney (8)	50
Fleur Garcia (8)	50
Jack Ormsby (9)	50
Harley Meadows (7)	51
Charley Rooke (8)	51
Bethany Kitchener (9)	51
Megan Jones (9)	52
Jonathan Brace (9)	52
Louise Cameron (9)	52
Hans Crusim (9)	53
April Ridgwell (8)	53
Stacey Vincent (8)	53
George Crawte (8)	54
Alicia Playll (8)	54
Coby Ferguson (8)	54
Evie Burke (8)	55
Paige Bashford (8)	55
Alice Rogers (9)	55
Lucy Franks-Jones (7)	56
Mark Morrison (9)	56
Rebecca Rees (8)	57
Lucy Goddard (8)	57
Thomas Jackson (8)	58
Bethany Howe (9)	58
Katie Ellis (7)	59
Dion Thomas (8)	59
Georgina Dunham (8)	60
Nicole Crowder (8)	60
Hannah Goode (8)	60
Oliver Armstrong (8)	61
Alice Halls (8)	61
Fawn Doggett (9)	61
Charlotte Clark (8)	62
Victoria Peet (7)	62
Elicia Draper (7)	62
Chloe Smith (8)	63
Sarah Bevan (9)	63
Charlotte Hurrell (9)	63
Daniel Hawkins (7)	64
Brody Thomson (9)	64
Madison McCandless (9)	64
Hayley Irwin (9)	65

Lauren Sumner (9)	65
Ashleigh Monk (7)	65
Rebecca Sumner (9)	66
Ryan Greenaway (9)	66
Jesse Caldwell (7)	67
Luke Jackson (9)	67
Rae-lee Coe (9)	68
Aimee Savill (7)	68
Raj Ranavaya (9)	68
Sam Lewis (10)	69
Alfie Marks (9)	69
Rowan Osborne (7)	69
Jade Hall (7)	70
George Bennett (7)	70
Nicole Kemp (9)	71
Harriet Dunwoody (9)	71
Lewis Sell (9)	72
Patricia Attwood (7)	72
Joshua Lao (9)	73
Liam Arnold (8)	73
Lauma Sarkane (9)	74
Lee Watts (7)	74
Chloe Starr (7)	75
Liam Stalley (9)	75
Alfie Summers (7)	76
Danielle Kidd (7)	76
Eleanor Seager (9)	76
Cameron Brown (7)	77
Isabella White (8)	77
Minh-Nhan Vo (8)	77
Matthew Snares (9)	78
Zack Perry Brace (8)	79
Korhelia Groralewska (8)	79
Jake Van Weede (7)	79
Harley Camp (9)	80
Pramita Gurung (7)	80
Bailey Ridlington (9)	80
Julia Belteki (7)	81
Mason McCandless (8)	81
Ashleigh-Jo Hare (9)	81
Tom Seager (7)	82
Olivia Alltree (8)	82

Joshua Weeks (7) — 83
Jonah Alltree (9) — 83
Tia Burrett (9) — 84
Oakleigh-Anne Brace (9) — 84
James Bovaird (7) — 85
Rachel Holland (9) — 85
T J Baker (10) — 86
Daniel Weeks (9) — 86
Nikita Schooling (9) — 87
Lauren Starr (9) — 87
Joshua Broughall (9) — 88
Rachael Sumner (9) — 88

La Salette Catholic Primary School
Billy Thomas (9) — 89

Montgomerie Junior School
Taylor Cranshaw (10) — 89
Caitlin Dellar (8) — 90
Tristan Lewis (8) — 90
Amy Sparrow (9) — 91
Tate Royer (9) — 91
Shannon Goodwin (10) — 92
Connor Tyler (9) — 92
Rosie Webster (9) — 93
Britney Lashmar (10) — 93
Alex Pate (9) — 94
William Taylor (9) — 94
Christopher Whitlock (9) — 95
Shannon Townsend (9) — 95
Samantha Doe (8) — 96
Michelle Sillitoe (8) — 96
Morgan Davies (8) — 97
Keeley Pitt-Stanley (9) — 97
Alice Lawrence (8) — 98
Luke Rock (9) — 99
Elle MacDonald (8) — 99
Patrick Mackinnon (8) — 100
Iona Shaw (9) — 100
Joshua Wiggins (9) — 101
Megan White (9) — 101

Elise Winning (8)	102
Hannah Broad (8)	103
Chloe Larkins (9)	104
Beth Healey (8)	105
Claudia Claydon (9)	106
Aaron Cole (9)	107
Anya Tobin (9)	107
Maddy McDonald (9)	108
Jodie Chong (8)	108
Joe Coster (9)	109
Bethany McCreath (8)	109
Ross Beckett (8)	110
Harry Fortt (8)	110
Jessica Dunmow (9)	111
Lilac Limacher (9)	111
Bradley Fuller (9)	112
Sidnie Wayman (9)	112
Ben Goringe (10)	113

Nazeing County Primary School

Amy Cannell (9)	113
Nicole Ciccarelli (9)	114

Perryfields Junior School

Jordan Dennis (10)	115
Liam Mears	115
Kianna Offord Pickering (8)	116
Emily Wood (10)	116
Eilish Pudney (10)	117
Tom Nash (11)	117
Elisha Bedding (11)	118
Alexandra Claire Simmons (11)	118
Megan Lea (9)	119
Ryan Shayler (11)	119
Millie Austin-Coskry (8)	120
Luke Clarke (10)	120
Samuel Ellingford-Frost (11)	121
Tyler Hadlow (11)	121
Georgina Ginnaw (10)	122
Charlotte Ginnaw (8)	122
Eric Austin-Coskry (10)	123

Daniel Owens (10)	123
Jack Kilbey (10)	124
Maddison Cowie (10)	125
Samuel Taylor (8)	125
Milly Drummond (10)	126
Tayla Johnson (10)	126
Joe Young (10)	127
Cameron Mear (10)	127
Jordan Magrath (8)	128
Jasmin Hardwick-Box (8)	128
Sam Templeman (11)	128
Amy Jacobs (8)	129
Holly Raymond	129
Alex Middlebrook (10)	129
Shailan Dhruv Gohil (11)	130
Jack Williamson (10)	130
Joseph Williams (9)	131
Lauren Shaw (9)	131
Mahlon King (10)	132
Sam Thompson (10)	132
Amy Brewster (11)	132
Gemma Wilson (8)	133
Georgia Robertson (8)	133
Paddy Wood (8)	133
Madeleine Bye (9)	134
Calum Wilson (11)	134
Sam Stuckey (8)	135
Cameron Stevenson (8)	135
Aaron Green (7)	136
Ashley Williams (10)	136
Molly Reid (9)	137
Robert White (8)	137
Shahzaib Shaikh (9)	138
Gemma Longman (8)	138
George Suttling (10)	138
Karun Mistry (10)	139
Campbell McLay-Kidd (9)	139
Megan Glover (7)	139
Adam Norton-Steele (8)	140
Courtney Drury (8)	140
Jack Johnson (10)	141
Georgia Bellsham (9)	141

Peter Gilbey (10)	142
Lauren Harris (10)	142
Artiom Evans (8)	142
Leah Coggins (7)	143
Adam Jacobs (10)	143
Jessica Carter (10)	143
Melissa Burton (8)	144
Lauren Clay (9)	144
Alicia Thompson (7)	145
Hannah Whiteley (10)	145
Morgan Matthams (8)	146
Charlotte Perkins (8)	146
Samuel Tregaskes (9)	147
Ben Gillyon (9)	147

St Antony's RC Primary School, Woodford Green

Conor J Sherlock (10)	147
Kelechi Ojiako (7)	148
Annabella King (11)	148
Charlotte Ring (9)	148
Jordan Grace (10)	149
Lydia Nugent (11)	149
Francesca Hill (10)	150
Olivia Gibson (10)	150
Louise Griffin (10)	150
Niamh Fitzgerald (11)	151

St Teresa's RC Primary School, Basildon

Melissa Foakes (10)	151
Tony Stewart (10)	151
Shelby Jarrett-Fenton (10)	152
Vicky Oshunremi (11)	152
Devon Sloley (10)	152
Georgia Anderson (10)	153
Deborah Shobande (10)	153
Zainab Williams (10)	154
Jack Anderson (10)	154
Ellie Nugent (10)	155
Judith Mason (10)	155
Fleur Campbell (10)	156
Matthew Spooner (10)	156

Hollie Magner (10)	157
Michael Tucker (10)	157
John Sagomba (10)	158
Ellen Smith (10)	158
Angel Hart (10)	159
Mitch Langley (11)	159
Brogan Morgan (10)	160
Sam Murray (10)	160

Wells Primary School

Alice Davidson (10)	161
Christy Gilbert (8)	161
Abigail Saffron (10)	162
Joseph Morgan (11)	162
Joe Philpott (9)	163
Geraldine Wan (9)	164
Elizabeth Stoney (7)	164
Joshua Fernandez-Steele (10)	165
Sarah Zheng (9)	165
Lydia Watkins (9)	166
Annie Cowen (7)	166
Divya Ramesh Arjan (7)	167
Eleanor Richardson (9)	168
Mia Berelson (10)	168
Georgia Roberts (8)	169
Laura Harvey (7)	169
Jessica Scott (7)	170
Noor Jamal (11)	170
Kitty Mae Atkins (10)	171
Lillian Delves (9)	171
Atif Siddiqui (10)	172
Louise Ranken (10)	173

The Poems

Grasshoppers

Like a bouncing ball, hopping up and down,
wandering through the grass.
As beautiful as the night sea, emerald, ruby,
Up and down the garden it hops and leaps,
in the fresh, graceful dew.
Jumping and joyful, as happy as a clown,
it hops round the night garden.

Jade Oliver (8)
Blenheim County Primary School

Scorpion

Your scorpion might be venomous and freaky.
Your scorpion might be a sand scorpion, prickly with a painful bite.
Your scorpion may be a spicy scorpion, with legs of anger.
Your scorpion might be a rock scorpion, blended in colour.

Kieran Halls (8)
Blenheim County Primary School

Buzz

Like a siren of noise she buzzes past,
Rushing to her home like lightning.
Collecting pollen from all over the world,
Whizzing home to feed her children well.

Abigail Last (9)
Blenheim County Primary School

Grasshoppers

Your grasshopper might be a dusky grasshopper,
small and pale.
Your grasshopper might be a forest grasshopper,
dark and wild.
Your grasshopper may be small and colourful,
with a cracking sound.
Your grasshopper may be a glowing grasshopper,
with a powerful jump.

Ellie Kavanagh (9)
Blenheim County Primary School

Grasshopper

Your grasshopper might be a meadow grasshopper,
emerald and lucky.
Your grasshopper might be a dusky grasshopper,
tiny and shiny.
Your grasshopper may be small and lively and jumpy.
Your grasshopper may be a forest grasshopper,
with a shrieking cry.

Chloe Williams (9)
Blenheim County Primary School

Dragonfly

Like a burning lantern,
Sparkling like an emerald jewel.
Like a siren of noise,
It rushes past you,
In the dark night,
It shines,
As the stars shine in front of you.

Mollie Chalkley (8)
Blenheim County Primary School

Grasshopper

Your grasshopper might be a sand grasshopper,
big and friendly.
Your grasshopper might be a dusky grasshopper,
cool and colourful.
Your grasshopper may be reflecting and luminous,
with a powerful jump.
Your grasshopper may be a garden grasshopper,
shrieking in joy.

Louis Chitticks (9)
Blenheim County Primary School

Grasshopper, Grasshopper

Your grasshopper might be a glowing grasshopper,
wierd and green.
Your grasshopper might be an autumn grasshopper,
emerald and shining.
Your grasshopper may be prickly and scary,
with a super hop.
Your grasshopper may be a garden grasshopper,
jumping far.

Jarrod Mullett (9)
Blenheim County Primary School

Grasshoppers, Grasshoppers

Your grasshopper might be a glowing grasshopper,
that glows like lightning.
Your grasshopper might be an autumn grasshopper,
colourful and pointy.
Your grasshopper may be green and bright, with a great jump.
Your grasshopper may be a dusky grasshopper that hops

Niamh Finnegan (8)
Blenheim County Primary School

Grasshopper, Grasshopper

Your grasshopper might be a glowing grasshopper,
green and lucky.
Your grasshopper might be an autumn grasshopper,
colourful and shimmering.
Your grasshopper may be a dusky grasshopper,
dull and grey, that jumps high.
Your grasshopper may be nasty and spiteful and sneaky.

Amy Eden (9)
Blenheim County Primary School

Dragonfly, Dragonfly

Dragonfly, dragonfly, as graceful as a dancer.
As elegant as the sunshine.
With a glassy back, black as coal.
The dragonfly swirls as delicate as a feather.
The dragonfly's eyes burn like a torch.

Storm Booth (9)
Blenheim County Primary School

The Ladybird

Ladybird
Like a red dot in the sky
Shimmering
Like a ruby
In the sunlight
Ladybird
Like a dream
Darker and darker
It hides its spots
As it drifts off into the moonlight.

Charlie Waterman-Walden (9)
Blenheim County Primary School

Grasshopper, Grasshopper

Your grasshopper might be an autumn grasshopper,
emerald and ruby.
Your grasshopper might be a sand grasshopper,
camouflaged and like a lizard.
Your grasshopper may be long and luminous,
with a quick scurry.
Your grasshopper may be a meadow grasshopper,
beautiful and glistening.

Joe Emberson (8)
Blenheim County Primary School

Grasshopper, Grasshopper

Your grasshopper might be a forest grasshopper,
ugly and prickly.
Your grasshopper might be a dusky grasshopper,
small and lucky.
Your grasshopper may be small and creepy,
with a great bounce.
Your grasshopper may be a sand grasshopper,
camouflaged, with a super jump.

Connor Andrews (9)
Blenheim County Primary School

Scorpions Of Death

Your scorpion might be a shipped scorpion,
spiky and venomous.
Your scorpion might be a sea scorpion,
enormous and fierce.
Your scorpion might be a desert scorpion,
hairy and dark.
Your scorpion might be a forest scorpion,
small and fast.

Ellis Misirlisoy (8)
Blenheim County Primary School

Dragonfly

Dragonfly
Like a dazzling diamond
Sparkling
Like a jewel
In daylight
Sunrise, it shines
As blue sapphires
Floating higher
Dragonfly
Like a beam of light
Flying
Like an eagle
In lightness
Daylight it shimmers
As dazzling as the water
Shining brighter.

Elspeth Macnab-Stark (9)
Blenheim County Primary School

Butterfly

Butterfly
Like a dazzling diamond
Sparkling
Like coloured lights
In sunshine
Daytime it flies
As glittering as stars
Glowing brighter.

Laura Moore (8)
Blenheim County Primary School

Spider

Spider
As black as the darkness.
Harmless
As hairy as a bear.
In blackest night it scurries,
As the cheetah,
Running faster.

Sonny Lock (8)
Blenheim County Primary School

Wow Grasshoppers

Grasshoppers
Like a jumping radio.
Green.
Like sparkling grass.
In the burning sun,
They shine.
As people walk by,
They jump up in joy.

Karis Nash (8)
Blenheim County Primary School

Spider

Like a black night
Hairy
As moving up the wall
It scuttles.

Sophie Phillips (8)
Blenheim County Primary School

Kitten

Kitten
Like a furry ball
Playful
Like a playful puppy
In light
Daytime, it plays
chasing a butterfly
Jumping higher.

Rebecca Nolan (8)
Blenheim County Primary School

Bees

Like the yellow sun
Shining
As high as
The clouds
In light
As the sky
Shimmering in daylight.

Charley Price (8)
Blenheim County Primary School

Butterfly

Butterfly
As elegant as the sunrise
Smooth and colourful
In daylight
They flutter in the sky
Soaring
Higher and higher.

Leticia Rigg (8)
Blenheim County Primary School

Panda

As long as a bamboo stick
Pimples
Like wings of steel
In daylight
Daylight it stashes
As a white whale
Growing bigger.

Connor Stephens (8)
Blenheim County Primary School

Dragonfly

Dragonfly
As beautiful as the sunshine
Shimmering
Like Heaven high above
In daylight
Daytime it flies
As dazzling as the water
As it flies higher.

Krysten Tobin (8)
Blenheim County Primary School

Snakes

Like a painted picture
In sunshine
Daylight it slithers
As the worm
Slithering slow.

Jack Andrews (9)
Blenheim County Primary School

Dragonfly

Dragonfly
As dazzling as the water
Sparkling
Like sparkling diamonds
In sunshine
Daytime as it glimmers
As the sun shines
Bright today.

Owen Treais (8)
Blenheim County Primary School

Dragonfly

Like a morning song
Sparkling
Like a jewel
In daytime
Sunset it flies
Like the graceful eagle
Soaring higher.

Emily Allen (8)
Blenheim County Primary School

Butterfly

Like a beautiful twilight
Like coloured rainbows
In the daylight
Sunrise it flies
As a diamond
Flying higher.

Danielle Burgess (8)
Blenheim County Primary School

Bee

Bee
Like the yellow sun
Buzzing
Like busy workers
In light
Morning it shines
As the sky
Shimmering in the light.

Alfie Cook (8)
Blenheim County Primary School

Black Spider

Black spider
Like a black night
Hairy
As moving up the wall
It's creeping in the night.

Faith Gensberg (8)
Blenheim County Primary School

Snakes

As smooth as a snake
Damp
As sticky as a snail
Slithering slowly
In the woods
In daylight
Weaving.

Jason Harrold (8)
Blenheim County Primary School

Butterfly

Butterfly
Like a shimmering ruby
Shimmering
Like breathtaking lights
In sunlight days it flits
Glittering like stars
Glowing brighter
Sparkling.

Kacey Holloway (8)
Blenheim County Primary School

Dragonfly

Dragonfly
As blue as sapphires
Dazzling
Like a diamond
In daytime
Sunrise it flies
Like a graceful eagle
Soaring higher.

Keith Hoang (8)
Blenheim County Primary School

Giant Squid

Giant squid
As long as ships
Swimming
Like a jellyfish
In the moonrise
Nightfall it hunts
As the moon falls
Going deeper.

Nicholas Harris (8)
Blenheim County Primary School

Dragonfly

Like a hummingbird
Buzzing
Like a crackling radio
In sunshine
In sunrise it flies
As a dazzling diamond
Flying higher
Dragonfly
Like coloured lights
Whizzing.
Like a jewel
In darkness
It sleeps
Like a morning song
Whizzing faster.

Lucy Johns (8)
Blenheim County Primary School

Personification

The sun is hidden,
While the grey clouds are crying.

The grass cuddles together,
To keep warm.

The school gate waits patiently,
For the cold caretaker to open them,
Creaking softly with rust.

The teddy bear snores after
a long day of being cuddled constantly
by the baby.

Adam Trinder (10)
Hacton Primary School

Saturday Morning

The car yawns and shudders
as it wakes up
to go to the park
on a crisp Saturday morning.

The trees whisper secret conversations
and the flowers laugh
at a joke the oak tree
made.

The clouds kiss high in the sky
and the lilies and roses do
the petal dance
in the cool, summer breeze.

The river ran by in a race
with the wind and the little baby seedling
drank and ate and grew and is now
a healthy, growing plant.

Jake Harris (10)
Hacton Primary School

How To Make A Monster

A head as round as a furry football,
A body as thin as a small twig,
Ears like big African elephant ears,
A mouth as big as the London Dungeons,
Teeth as sharp as needles,
Eyes like red balls of flame,
Legs and arms as long as the pillars
On the Queen's Bridge,
Claws like sharp pencils,
A tail as small as a pig's.

Ben Hatton (10)
Hacton Primary School

My Sister

My sister is a lovely one
She would always help me
And if she needed help
I would help her too.

She loves me so much
And I love her too
We get along nicely
But not every day.

Sometimes I help her
With her homework
Or sometimes she
Helps me.

Normally she goes to sleep
When she was little
She used to bite, but not now
She is nice and caring.

Chloe Fordham (10)
Hacton Primary School

Arsenal

The best team plays in red and white,
When I watch them I'm full of delight,
Thierry Henry left and I had a frown
For weeks and weeks I felt very down.

When they score I shout out loud,
To win the league I would be very proud
I dream to play for them one day, with all the fans
Shouting, 'Pownall hooray!'

Gareth Pownall (10)
Hacton Primary School

The Classroom

The tray sits happily,
In the shade,
Under the desk,
Lazily sleeping.

The desks are happily waiting,
Strong and ready,
For when the children come
In and start writing.

The chairs rest,
Building up strength,
For when the class
Of noisy children
Come and sit on them.

The cubes lay in their boxes,
Waiting for maths,
So they can get out
And stretch their legs.

Pencils sit in their pots,
Waiting to be switched
For a different one,
They yawn as they wait.

The board sits
Ready and waiting
For the projector to be switched on,
After the children have arrived.

The calculators sit,
Bunched up in their
Cramped caddy, waiting
To be used, to solve problems.

Cassie Finch (10)
Hacton Primary School

The Library

The old armchair
Heaves a great sigh
As the dust dances around
On the dipping seat.

The piano
Plays a soft tune
And closes his eyes
And goes to sleep.

The little rug
On the wooden floor
Merely sits there, waiting
For morning to come.

All the teacups
And saucers gather together
For a meeting and chatter
Amongst themselves.

The old book whispers words of his own
Fairy tale that
Was forgotten.

The beautiful chandelier
Hangs from the ceiling
All the tiny crystals
Getting partners and dancing together.

Sophia Harris (10)
Hacton Primary School

My Lovely Gran

She is an old, soft armchair, covered in silky material
And a white horse taking you everywhere
She is a sunflower swinging in the breeze
She is a morning person, waking up at 6am in the morning.
She is the warm month of March, when all the new flowers come out.
She is a character called Mary Poppins
She is a smart Bentley car.

Taylor Kearney (10)
Hacton Primary School

My Family

My nan is always there for me, wherever I will be
She is the greatest nan in the whole wide world
She's like a mum to me.

My dad is quite far away
I think of him all day
He's got a dog called Bozy
Who is extremely noisy

My nanny Jean is very clean
And active and extreme
She is alive and she's 75

My grandad is a handy man
A clever man indeed
If you have a problem
Just call my grandad Steve!

Frankie is at university
A teacher she will be
Teaching children A B C
And others how to read

My dog is my pride and joy
She barks all day long
And she's not as small as she seems.

Chloe White (10)
Hacton Primary School

Untitled

On the pitch they come to play
One team home and one away.
Home team in red, away team in green,
At the beginning nice and clean.

The game begins and the whistle blows,
No more smiley faces are shown.
The ball is passed from man to man,
Cheers and jeers from every fan.

Half-time over and still no score
And green fans moaning,
It should be four.

The pitch was wet,
The reds soon kicked into the net.
Last five minutes, let's hope it's quick,
The greens have been awarded a penalty kick!

The game was a draw, not a bad score.

Daniel Coombs (10)
Hacton Primary School

My Dad

He is a big sofa, he is hard to sit on but
comfortable.
He is a giant, hairy gorilla.
He is the beginning of a warm October.
He isn't sporty.
He is one of the pigs out of 'The Three Little Pigs',
because he is smart.
He is a grey milkman's van.
He is a big, redwood tree.

Danny Wallace (10)
Hacton Primary School

A Poem About Animals

Cute as a baby,
Soft as a teddy,
Fussy like my little sister,
Hypo like me.

Spotty like Dalmatians,
Brown as wood,
Wild as foxes,
Faster than cars.

Prickles as sharp as needles,
Spiky like a hairbrush,
Small as a shoe,
Eaten by foxes.

They're noisy, like a drill,
They're a sun in water,
Splish, splash they go,
Orange feet like satsumas on sticks.

Shannon Morton (10)
Hacton Primary School

At Upton Park

West Ham, West Ham
We think you are
Great and you're better than all the rest

We have beaten all the
Rest of them, so players come
And join the best

You wear the colours
Of claret and blue so
Wear the kit with pride

For all the Hammers young
And old are still
Standing singing side by side.

Jay Cappleman (10)
Hacton Primary School

Seasons

Walking home in the snow
Gives your cheeks a chilly glow.
Blustery winds and heavy rain
Oh my goodness, what a pain!

Daffodils in the sun
Makes you want to skip and run.
Bunnies hopping here and there,
Children playing at a fair.

Picnics on a sandy beach
Are suddenly within your reach.
Children screaming, having fun,
Everybody in the sun.

Autumn leaves falling down
All the conkers on the ground.
Crunchy leaves beneath your feet,
As you walk along the street.

Sally Cleary (11)
Hacton Primary School

The Sleepy Snowdrop

Silently, creeping upwards
the sleepy snowdrop rises
Softly lifting its pretty head
to show off its beauty.

Its delicate petals drooping down,
sitting in bright, white snow
The ice-cold wind blows through it
as it takes a breath of fresh air.

Louise Crockford (10)
Hacton Primary School

Millie

Millie is a beagle,
She has eyes like an eagle.
Black, brown or white
She likes to take flight.

She buries her bone,
To make sure it's her own.
She eats everything in sight
From morning till night.

We grab her lead
After her feed,
She begins to bark
As we drive down to the park.

When we come home
She doesn't sleep alone,
She curls up in a ball,
Goodnight all.

Amy Miller (10)
Hacton Primary School

Dad

Your dad,
Can make you mad,
But there's goodness inside a man,
Just like the taste of ham,
Sometimes he's king of the TV,
But just let him be,
Because I love my dad
And he loves me.

Amber Cundall (10)
Hacton Primary School

My Poem On My Family

My dad:
My dad is great,
He's also my mate.
He never leaves anything on his plate
And for that reason he's overweight!

My mum:
My mum is like a friend to me,
She helps me understand you see.
When I come home from school at night,
She helps me get my homework right!

My nan and grandad:
My nan and grandad are so kind,
A better pair you would not find.
They treat me with sweets and money,
But most of all they are so funny!

My sister:
My sister is a football fan,
She goes to watch it when she can.
She nearly likes it as much as me,
That's why we get on so well you see!

Me:
I'm the youngest of our clan,
And I am an avid Arsenal fan.
I like to kick a ball or two,
Writing this poem was hard work, *phew!*

Daniel Powell (10)
Hacton Primary School

Fruit And Veg

Apples sitting in assembly, all together
In a line, not making a bit of sound.

Carrots are like fingers,
Long and pointy and thin.

Cherries are like red,
Shiny, bouncy balls.

Banana is like someone smiling,
Because they are happy.

Shars Jerke (10)
Hacton Primary School

Untitled

Mars is a shiny red
cricket ball,
gleaming in
the solar system.

Jupiter is a giant
beach ball,
spinning and floating
among the stars.

Pluto is a
golf ball,
smaller than
them all.

Earth is a
blue and green
football.
Where
we live.

Jimmy Marriner (10)
Hacton Primary School

My Poem

Plays with number 9,
Should play for England,
Scoring all the time,
Plays for West Ham, who is he?

Number 32, for Man U,
Signed in the summer, 2007,
Used to play for West Ham too,
Who is he?

Plays for England and Chelsea,
Wears 8 for both sides,
One best midfielder, may get injured,
Who is he?

Best centre forward ever,
Plays with number 14, can't tell club,
Used to play Premiership,
Who is he?

Bobby James (11)
Hacton Primary School

My Mum

She is a beautiful, elegant dressing table
Covered in silk,
And a hot summer day.
She is the hot month of July,
And the warm sunrise of the morning.
She is very expensive Jimmy Choo shoes!
She is a warm chocolate-coated marshmallow,
And a slinky, shiny, new Honda Civic driving down a country lane,
She is a red rose, blooming with love,
And a robin flying around in the snow.

Grace Redwood (10)
Hacton Primary School

Tilly Lilly

My little Tilly Lilly
Is so very silly
Cute and pretty as can be
But so naughty you see.

Broccoli, apple, banana and carrot
She loves a tasty treat
On her wheel she runs all night
Until the early morning light.

In the hall she likes to run
On her way, following Mum
At the corner of the hall
She makes her great escape.

In her bed she wants to snuggle
Only after a great big cuddle
Every night, cosy and warm
That's my hamster, Tilly Lilly.

Emma Roberts (10)
Hacton Primary School

My Baby Sister

Connie is my baby sister,
She cries when she has a blister,
I love her a lot,
Although she's my little dot.

My baby sister is the best,
She's really cute in her vest,
She loves to play,
Every single day.

Megan Wilson-Storey (11)
Hacton Primary School

The Fog

The sky turned grey,
There was a white mist,
All of a sudden I felt damp,
There was no wind,
No sun, no nothing.
My hands went cold,
The fog was here,
I ran inside,
I tried to look out of the window,
But there was so much fog I couldn't see.
I had a dream about the fog that night,
In the morning I could see the light,
The fog had gone, *oh no, oh why?*
I cried as I stepped outside in the light.

Rebecca Howell (9)
Hacton Primary School

Untitled

It's yellow and you can eat it
But before eating it you have to peel it.
It's bendy as a sausage
Monkeys love to eat them too
Who am I?

You can drive me
I have four wheels
I need an engine to work me
You can sit in me
And I have a steering wheel
Who am I?

Abbie Gay (10)
Hacton Primary School

Snow, Snow And More Snow

It was an icy day
At the beginning of May,
All the children say,
'Can we go out to play?'
But inside they must stay.

The freezing cold air,
The children gaze in a stare,
The teacher also fixed a glare,
Now the school seemed like a lair,
Cold, but they didn't care.

The children needed a lift,
They were all in a drift,
The children were all bored stiff,
Inside they stare at a cliff,
In fact they all started telling myths.

Renée Dacres (10)
Hacton Primary School

The Fog

The fog, the fog is very damp
It looks like you have just woken up
You couldn't see the school
Or hardly any trees
You could just see the tree outside school
It was like the winter
It was like 6 o'clock in the morning
If you just looked out the window it looked cold
The floor was very damp and a bit muddy
It was very bleary like it had sunglasses
You could just about see the teacher
Then we came in and wrote about it.

Aaron Bolton (9)
Hacton Primary School

In The Park

The statue sighs after
Standing still all day,
The silent caretaker
Of the park.

The moon and
Stars play hide
And seek, the moon
Hides behind the clouds.

The leaves whisper
To each other
Rustling softly
In the wind.

Daisies quietly close
Their buds, waiting
Patiently for dawn's
Cold, first light.

The moon peeks out from behind
The cloud, only to be
Chased away by the sun
She hid behind a hill to
Wait for today's dusk.

The statue once more becomes rigid
The stars fade away
The leaves all whisper, 'Good morning,'
Daisies open again
The day has begun.

Jessica Lovell (10)
Hacton Primary School

My Brother

He is a soft but springy chair
He is a tiger looking for its prey
He is a Venus flytrap, because he is fast
He is a night person because he's awake
He is the warm month of May
He is Sully from Monsters Inc
He is a 5 star centre midfielder and captain
He is a Ferrari going 200mph
He is black, because he is smart.

Aran Güner (10)
Hacton Primary School

The 6PS Classroom

The chairs are waiting,
Waiting for morning,
When the noisy children come in
And wake them up.

The tables are stiff,
The tables are still,
Waiting for the work to be finished,
And will not jog the children until they are finished.

The cubes are sleeping,
Until needed, they are sleeping,
In maths sets they wake up,
Waiting to be used.

The books are lying,
Lying on the shelves snoring,
Waiting to be picked up,
But if not some play with their friends.

Sean Faulkner (10)
Hacton Primary School

Fruit And Veg

Carrots are like
Darts, flying through
The air, hitting
The target

Bananas, they are
Like the moon in
The way they're
Shaped, the man in the moon

Cherries, red as
Roses, sweet as
Sherbet, but
As juicy as strawberries.

Sam Jeffs (10)
Hacton Primary School

My Friend

She is a new, comfortable sofa covered
In leather,
She is a soft, gentle rabbit, running
around the field.
She is a big bunch of bright red roses
in someone's beautiful garden,
She is a lovely, calming April,
She is Hermione, brave and clever,
She is a bright pink, Smart Car, shooting
down the motorway.
She is a good dancer, dancing on the
West End stage.

Molly Sparks (11)
Hacton Primary School

The Forest

The moon hides when
The wolves howl.

The stick cries
When rubbing
Against his
Friend, trying to
Make fire.

The trees blink
When hikers come
With their torches, on
Their midnight hikes.

Mustafa Khraishi (11)
Hacton Primary School

The Classroom

The table
Waits quietly,
Before it has to hold
All the equipment.

The pen
Dawdles slowly,
Across the page
Before its work shift ends.

The book
Sits there,
To be opened so it can see
The sunlight and have breakfast.

The tray
Sleeps quietly,
Underneath the desk,
Until woken in the morning.

Luke Bolton (11)
Hacton Primary School

Our School

Our school is cool,
And it has a swimming pool,
You count to seven,
You'll be like you're in Heaven.
You learn about bones,
But you're not allowed phones.
Your friends are kind,
When you lose something and can't find.
We go there five days a week,
In class you're not allowed to shriek!

Aycin Kaya (9)
Hacton Primary School

The Plant

The plant comes out to say hello
The sun comes out moments later
And waits for flowers to face him.

The plant closes up
'Cause the moon came out
So he said to the sun, goodnight.

When all the plants come out
They all faced the sun
Then they all opened up
And yawned.

The roots were finding water
And the flowers were blinking
At the sun
The bees were getting pollen
And a bud was bursting into a flower.

Alex Wheeler (10)
Hacton Primary School

A Foggy Day

It was a foggy day
We weren't allowed to play
We had to wear mittens
As fluffy as kittens
I couldn't see the field
It was as clear as a white shield
A slight breeze
Made me sneeze.
That was a foggy day.

Laura Wood (9)
Hacton Primary School

The Fog

The sky was grey
The clouds were gone
There was a mist
I fell in a pile of mud
With my best bud
There was a dog in the fog
It tripped over a log.

Joseph Triggs (9)
Hacton Primary School

The Fog

I'm standing here in the fog
In the distance I can see a log
The fog is misty, hard to see
And also I almost walked into a tree
But as the mist clears away
I realise it's the start of the day.

Charlie Howsego (9)
Hacton Primary School

My Dad

He is a black, leather sofa
A big tiger in the jungle
He is a rose standing out in the garden
He is a hot June on a summer morning
He is one angry Range Rover going round the city.

Devon Perkins (10)
Hacton Primary School

The Foggy Day

It was a foggy day,
When the dew was about to lay,
You couldn't see a thing,
But the bells made a ding.
It was very cold,
The sun was gleaming gold,
A slight breeze
Made us all wheeze.
We could see the tree,
I saw a little bee.
That was the foggy day.

Peter Martin (10)
Hacton Primary School

The Blossom

The cherry blossom opens its body
On the first day of spring and breathes deeply
But still cold from the winter.

The wind sighs deeply
As the trees dance in the moonlight.

Rylan Purnell (10)
Hacton Primary School

The Fog

I came out of the door
And started to walk down
To the end of the field
I could not see anything
It was like looking down
at a floor of sparkling ice,
As the sun was just rising
you could feel the fog in your hands
It was like you were touching
an invisible, soft pillow
the grass was like a swimming pool
had just exploded all over the grass
You could feel the cold touch on
your arms and legs,
But it started to clear up.

Elisha Seymour (9)
Hacton Primary School

A Foggy Day

When I walk out
All you can see is mist
It's cold, dark
You can barely see
The mist is wet, airy
Turn around it's really soggy
Dark clouds gather
You feel like it's going to rain
I feel a shiver in my bones
You come in
Now it's warm.

Caitlin Dible (9)
Hacton Primary School

The Rain Fog

Rain, rain, rain,
Cold, cold rain.
The rain is so wet,
That I think I'm going
to sweat.
I think that the rain is so heavy,
because it tastes like cherry
and the rain is going to push me down the hole
because
I'm a big fool.
The rain is faster than ever,
because it's really clever.
The rain is going to push me down the pool,
because I'm a big baboon.
The rain is so wet that it made me explode,
But then it went away.

Edward Vulpe (9)
Hacton Primary School

Foggy Friday

As thick as ice,
Like 1,000 white dice,
It was a Friday,
Like no other day,
The frost was in the air,
Say goodbye to the Mayor
No more funfair after this night!
But there is still a glint of light.

Alex Secular (9)
Hacton Primary School

Snow Is Falling

Snow, snow, snow, snow is falling,
as soft as a kitten, on your mitten
Santa flying high
Up in the night sky

He looks at the children's lists
In the great foggy mist
Will he stay
Or will he fly away?

Do you believe in him?
Well if you do
You will get something
That might say moo!

Alex Cordaro (9)
Hacton Primary School

Our School

Our school is cool
and the boys play football,
you have lots of fun
when you count to one,
we count to seven
and wish for Heaven,
you learn about bones
and electricity like phones,
you learn RE
also PE.

Dean Wedge (9)
Hacton Primary School

The Fog

I came out the classroom door
And I couldn't even see my hand
I could feel the fog in my hands
Then I walked to the end of the field
I couldn't see my friends
It was spooky.

Lewis Bennett (9)
Hacton Primary School

Little Robin

Quick, quiet robin in the tree
Please come down and stay with me.
Little robin don't rush your food
You have loads of time.
Little robin you sing beautifully
But you are a wild animal.
Little, quick, quiet, cute robin
Stay where you are.
I must leave you before the night is done.
Little robin I must go, but did you know
When you need me just knock on my window
Then you'll be able to play with me.
Little robin you don't need to fear
That was just a suggestion.
Quick, quiet robin sitting in the tree
Please come down and stay with me.

Taylor Smith (7)
John Perry Primary School

Untitled

Strong, leafy tree, swaying in the breeze
There's a silver birch and seed trees.
Bare tree, oak tree and a chestnut tree
A large green tree is as bendy as a ruler
And as high as a house.
I love their smell and I love to hear them
Swaying in the wind.
I also love the way the bark is all rough and tough.
Look at the leafy sap tree
It looks like a redwood
And over there is another one
But this one is as big as a block of flats.
Look there's a birch tree.
That one's prickly and that one's thorny.
That trunk is so fat and wide.

Ellie Patience (8)
John Perry Primary School

Untitled

A beautiful butterfly is like
a flying propeller in the sunny sun,
Dancing in the moonlight and looking like a frog.
Helping everybody.
Flutter, flutter, go the big, blue wings in the moonlight.
Flash, flash.
Flowers have died,
but the butterfly does not die until Christmas
When the snow falls deep in the cold,
ice-blue and white snowy snow.
It's cold in the Arctic Ocean.

Joshua Ratford (7)
John Perry Primary School

Apple

Nice and good, shiny, crunchy, juicy apples
Bad and brunchy, black and brown apple.
Good red and green apple.
Green apple in the tree, on the outside branch.
No one can get the apple, tasty, juicy.
It tastes ripe.
Some people don't like apples, but I do.
There are apples that you can't eat
But if you do eat one you will get tummy ache.
Bad apples are not good for you.
Apples can help you to get moving
And you get your work done.
Fruit salad has apple in it.
Some apples are too ripe and not very nice.
People are getting healthy from apples.

Bethany Livesey (7)
John Perry Primary School

Untitled

Fluttering, flapping butterfly
that looks so colourful and delicate.
Butterfly, butterfly, swooshing, swaying.
Butterfly, butterfly, flying in the sky
so beautiful to watch all day.
Has lots of wings
the wings are smooth and soft,
softer than cotton wool.
Big spots for eyes and silky to touch
I could hold a butterfly all day long.

Cheyenne Borg (7)
John Perry Primary School

Untitled

A flying butterfly, fluttering in the air.
A flying, colourful, delicate butterfly flying in the trees.
A lovely, beautiful, delicate butterfly flying around my head.
A flapping, colourful, delicate butterfly flying towards me.
A fluttering, delicate butterfly trapped in a cage.
A wonderful, bright, colourful butterfly in my house.
A tired butterfly lifting so high in the sky.
A wonderful butterfly, lifting from rock to rock.

Brooke Shore (7)
John Perry Primary School

Untitled

Snake people can hear meee.
Slimy, hissing, along the grass.
Cobra, python, viper snakes
Sitting on a log.
A scaly snake.
The adder and a python snake fighting
Sss went the python snake.

Chloe Moore (7)
John Perry Primary School

Pine

Pine trees and apple trees.
Pear trees and plum trees.
Lots of tall trees swishing in the wind.
Green leaves dropping from the trees.
Some trees have a house in them.
Some trees give sap.
Birds nest in the trees and live in them.

Jessica-Anne Manning (7)
John Perry Primary School

The Butterfly

The butterfly always flutters away when people go near
Beautiful, loving and caring and butterflies are fair as well
The butterflies are very, very delicate
Butterflies are very, very symmetrical on the wings
The butterflies go around the flowers
To collect nectar with their tongues
The butterflies keep flapping and flapping their wings very fast.

Emily Brett (7)
John Perry Primary School

Snake

Snake slithering through a desert.
A poisonous snake, killing its prey.
A green grass snake trying to kill its prey.
I see and hear a rattlesnake hissing at me.
I can feel a back bendy snake on my feet.
I can see a cobra in the desert.
I can hear an adder snake sliding and slithering on the ground.

Harry Addison (7)
John Perry Primary School

Trees

Strong trees and weak trees
Bared trees and leafed trees
What can I see?
Blowing every leaf, some rustle so I can hear.
Some trees are as bendy as a plastic ruler
And some are as big as a block of flats
I can hear lots of leaves rustling in the trees
I like the sound of rustling leaves
Redwoods are the biggest trees, but they are in Canada.

Joe Sullivan Sparks (7)
John Perry Primary School

Untitled

Come and grant my wish tonight
Twinkly, glittery star so high
Try to catch them, you would not try.
Beautiful, golden sparkle in my eye.
Shining bright, shooting high,
Shooting stars are my favourites.
I see all the sparkling stars at night.
They're very bright, so high.
Make them come down, you would not try
If you like glitter look at stars.
Make a wish every night upon a star.

Mollie Wilson (7)
John Perry Primary School

Untitled

A hissing, moving snake on the grass.
Slimy, scaly, slow, scary, sly, slippery snake
On the green grass.
I can see 20 snakes on the grass.
As slimy as a snail.
As scaly as a human.

Colourful patterns
Slimy, long, bendy, slow, noisy, wiggly,
poisonous, frightening, slithery,
venomous types, hunting, coiled.
Cobra, grass, python, water,
Diamond, rattle, viper, adder.

I can feel a slimy snake.
I can see snakes all over the world.
I can hear a snake in the big jungle
Moving around.

Matthew Ramsden (7)
John Perry Primary School

Skipping Rope

A skipping rope is as fast as a cheetah
It goes slap on the floor when I skip with it
It is a super speedy skipping rope
Skipping with it makes me happy
I love skipping with my super speedy
Skipping rope, in the garden
It is as colourful as a butterfly
It is also long as a giraffe
Anyone could skip with it
It's a magical skipping rope
The skipping rope is fantastic
Marvellous skipping is my favourite thing
Is it yours?

Abbie Maulkerson (7)
John Perry Primary School

Untitled

A
golden
shooting
star twinkling
above the
sky. The golden touch of the sprinkly
day. I see then a shooting star twinkling up high
in the sky. A silver, glittery shooting star
As golden as a diamond.
A reaching star
in the
sky
sparkling
up
high.

Joy A Utonwanne (7)
John Perry Primary School

Untitled

A butterfly
as light as a piece of paper
Floating through the air.
A butterfly's beautiful blue wing
As fragile as a glass bottle.
A butterfly is as small as a red ant.
A beautiful big butterfly
Beating its white wings.

Kane Hearn
John Perry Primary School

Ice Cream

I love ice cream
It is so luscious and lovely.
A whole lot of it tastes good
When days are hot.
In a cone or on a dish
Or even with pie
Would be my wish
Vanilla, chocolate or rocky roll.

Macey Rees
John Perry Primary School

My Cat

A cat is like
a cuddly teddy bear
When she sits
on my lap.
I love my cute and soft
little cat.

Shelby Pickering (7)
John Perry Primary School

Butterfly

Beautiful butterfly beating her gorgeous wings
She's like a rainbow
Falling from the sky
Dancing butterfly,
Dancing around and around and around
She's a nice creature too
Good butterfly you have the gift of a baby butterfly
You are so delicate
You will soon be mine.

Tegan Churchill (7)
John Perry Primary School

Rhino

People charger
Massive horner
Heavy wader
Tree destroyer
Strong header
Big feeter
Bone muncher.

Reece Jackson (8)
Katherine Semar Junior School

T-Rex

Bone crusher
Massive teether
Giant stamper
Strong clawer
Human muncher
Scary monster
House destroyer
Animal eater.

Craig Carey (9)
Katherine Semar Junior School

Hallowe'en, Trick Or Treat

At Hallowe'en you get sweets
and spiders jump on you.
Be very scared of the ghostly people
or the people with pointy hats.

It's all inky dark outside.
Say trick or treat or else!
That's the rule of Hallowe'en.

Jessica Jozunas (8)
Katherine Semar Junior School

Cat

Furry wiggler
Slow eater
Food gobbler
Mouse catcher
Sneaky scratcher
Paw licker.

Jade Hunt (8)
Katherine Semar Junior School

Bees

Honey lover
First winner
Flying wiggler
Cross chaser
Speed stinger
Running hunter
Honey maker
Leg acher.

Nathan Richardson (8)
Katherine Semar Junior School

Best Friend

Swinging jumper
Cheeky banana
Banana gobbler
Crazy leaper
Tail curler
Furry cuddler
Constant chatterer.

Almas Ahmed (8)
Katherine Semar Junior School

My Budgie

Annoying speaker
Far flyer
Slow walker
Mean biter
Finger sitter
Cool colour
Loud sleeper
Crazy talker.

Conor McCabe (8)
Katherine Semar Junior School

Elephant

Huge stomper
Great bumper
Strong mover
Big jumper
Grey colour
Nut cruncher
Slow runner.

Bryony Wright (8)
Katherine Semar Junior School

Football

F ootball is my thing
O ver the goalie's head - a goal
O pen goal - a gift
T ackle their number five - it's my ball
B oots kick the ball - yes a goal!
A or B team, which one will I be picked for?
L egs are for running and playing football with
L inesmen wave their flags, he's offside!

Callum Courtney (8)
Katherine Semar Junior School

Butterfly

Brightly coloured
Big-winged flyer
Flower lover
High flyer
Amazing colours
Camouflaged flutterer.

Fleur Garcia (8)
Katherine Semar Junior School

Dog

Fast runner
Loud barker
Tail chaser
Nice colour
Hairy monster
Funny joker
Loud panter
Food cruncher

Jack Ormsby (9)
Katherine Semar Junior School

My Magical Place

I saw a pink castle,
with trees and golden plums
around it.
With whispering breezes
and butterflies
fluttering by.
Oh look there's Mickey Mouse
walking happily by.

Harley Meadows (7)
Katherine Semar Junior School

Dog

Dog hunter
Bone lover
Paw licker
Fast runner
Friendly pal
Bark maker
Dog barker.

Charley Rooke (8)
Katherine Semar Junior School

Dolphin

Elegant leaper
Fast swimmer
People lover
Smiley creature
Bluey colour
Fun player
Fish eater.

Bethany Kitchener (9)
Katherine Semar Junior School

The Sea Of Ice
(Inspired by 'The Sea of Ice' by Casper David Friedrich)

I n the ice beneath,
C rushed by sharp teeth,
E vil ice opened,

S hip been broken,
H ere in the sea,
I ce snapped in half,
P lease don't laugh!

Megan Jones (9)
Katherine Semar Junior School

The Sea Of Ice
(Inspired by 'The Sea of Ice' by Casper David Friedrich)

The ship is trapped in an icy war,
With shields, swords and all,
With people dying all around,
With daggers all around to kill.

With mess all around them,
The ship lies deserted,
All around there is calm,
The war is over and done.

Jonathan Brace (9)
Katherine Semar Junior School

My Mum

M y mum is wicked
Y ou're very cool.

M y mum kisses me before bed.
U nder the water we swim.
M y mum is the best mum in the world.

Louise Cameron (9)
Katherine Semar Junior School

Dragon, Dragon Slayers

D is for darkness
R is for roaming in the darkness
A is for army of dragons
G is for magnificent gate of dragons
O is for over war
N is for nation of the dragons
S is for slayer of dragons.

Hans Crusim (9)
Katherine Semar Junior School

The Black Cat

The black cat sat on a top hat
The black cat jumped on a mat
The black cat saw a rat
The black cat sat on a top hat
And jumped on a mat and saw a rat
Run out of the cat flap.

April Ridgwell (8)
Katherine Semar Junior School

Monkey

High jumper
Fast mover
Quick leaper
Grey nibbler
Small streaker
Grape crusher
Funny chatterer
Mess maker.

Stacey Vincent (8)
Katherine Semar Junior School

Football

F is for friends who play football with me
O is for over the keeper's head. *Goooal!*
O is for juice fresh oranges you gobble at half-time
T is for terrific free kicks, Drogba style
B is for brilliant goals by top class players
A is for amazing corners which curl like a cat
L is for lucky saves by a keeper from penalties, reaction of a shark
L is for Lampard, a brilliant Chelsea star.

George Crawte (8)
Katherine Semar Junior School

Nails

Some nails are rough and some nails are smooth
When they move they are elegant like a dancer
It's a bit stinky when you use nail varnish!
There are many different colours, like a rainbow
I don't like my sister's nails they're short and stubby
Nails, nails, short and long
They just grow and grow and grow until they get long.

Alicia Playll (8)
Katherine Semar Junior School

Bears

The bear in the woods is hairy and his name is Beary
He's big and caring and a little bit scary
He has sharp teeth and big paws
And glaring eyes and pointy sharp claws
So watch out if you go down to the woods today!

Coby Ferguson (8)
Katherine Semar Junior School

Firework Night

Fireworks bang, crash, and shake up in the sky.
They whizz and pop and whirl and fly.
The Catherine wheel spins round, like a dog chasing its tail.
The colours are beautiful, red, blue and yellow.
Watch out it's going up, then it booms up in the air.
Take care of the sparklers dancing all around.
Finally comes the bonfire, hot like a furnace,
With its flames like tongues in the air.

Evie Burke (8)
Katherine Semar Junior School

A-tishoo

There was a girl called Millie
Her favourite flower was lilies.
There was one problem though,
She sneezed every time she went near them, so
She stayed away until she found a friend,
He was called Billy but he bought her some lilies . . .
A-tishoo!

Paige Bashford (8)
Katherine Semar Junior School

The Seaside

S is for the sunny days
E is for everyone who goes for a swim
A is for a child having fun
S is for swimming that everyone loves
I is for icy cold sea in the winter
D is for children digging in the sand
E is for everyone who is having fun!

Alice Rogers (9)
Katherine Semar Junior School

The Magical Garden Of Wonders

Bumblebees, sucking pollen out of colourful plants
Squirrels scampering up a tall tree
Daisies popping out of the golden ground

In the freezing start of winter, the ponds are full of fish
Happy, some sad, lots graceful and extremely poisonous

Nuts from every branch, low enough to collect

In spring the beautiful flowers are filled with happiness
And delight to see the sun again
While dragonflies are hovering around the garden

It's summer now, and the trees are nice and bushy
Butterflies flitting to and fro
And in the pond there are lilies

Finally autumn, with golden leaves falling to the ground

Last of all winter,
Everything is covered with clear, crystal snow.

And on and on and on . . .

Lucy Franks-Jones (7)
Katherine Semar Junior School

Dragon

The dragon's very brave.
He lives in a smelly cave.
He's got a very long tail.
Even when he eats the mail.
His wings are so very gold.
The most dangerous or so he's been told.
His tail is very spiky.
His nickname is Mikey.
He breathes out purple fire.
From the dragon world he never wants to retire.

Mark Morrison (9)
Katherine Semar Junior School

Colours

Colours, colours, everywhere, they're so beautiful.
As amazing as diamonds, rubies and sapphires.
Colours in pictures, colours in patterns.
There are colours in hats, on beaches and colours anywhere you go,
Farms or zoos.
There are colours in rainbows and colours in sunsets.
Sweets have colours, so does chocolate.
There are colours within the sea,
Colours surrounding the sun, on rocks and snow.

Red, blue, green, yellow, white, black, grey, brown,
gold, silver, purple, pink, indigo, see-through, navy.

Rebecca Rees (8)
Katherine Semar Junior School

My Teacher

My teacher sits at her desk
Drinking tea, staring at her laptop,
Funny as can be.
Sitting in her chair pointing at me,
Teacher, teacher I hurt my knee!

My teacher is very kind
She can find anything, she really doesn't mind.
My teacher is the very best
But if you touch her desk,
She'll tickle you to death!

Lucy Goddard (8)
Katherine Semar Junior School

Vampires

Vampires come in all shapes and sizes.
Some fat and some skinny.
Vampires are scary and fast.
They have blood on their teeth.

Some run fast and slow.
Vampires are as scary as lions.
Vampires are great big pests!

Some are strong and muscly.
Some are not very strong.
They creep around cities and villages.
They are really naughty.
They are very tall.

Thomas Jackson (8)
Katherine Semar Junior School

On The Melting Candle

On the melting candle
I see some wax.

By the melting candle
I see some light.

On the melting candle
I see some flame.

On the melting candle
I see in the flames red, white, blue.

By the light of the melting candle
I see me and you.

Bethany Howe (9)
Katherine Semar Junior School

Swan Meadow

There is glowing grass and whispering trees
That sing in the breeze
A gentle stream flows by
With lovely green lily pads and water flowers
A big tree, with blossom, growing high
It leans over the stream

People in canoes come rowing by every day
Lots of people admire it
The trees shine in the sun
The birds sing a lovely tune as they glide by
Leaves come dazzling down slowly
They get brushed by the wind.

Katie Ellis (7)
Katherine Semar Junior School

The Baby Dragon

In the big castle there is a playful dragon,
as small as a sparrow.
With his dad
they dance and roar every night
and sunbathe every day.
when they go to sleep they snore,
like drums bashing together.
Never brush their teeth because . . .
Snap! They bite!

Dion Thomas (8)
Katherine Semar Junior School

Summer Holidays

Summer holidays are playful, energetic and fun
The children run free under the big, hot sun.
Mothers go out shopping for school shoes and stuff
While pop stars go to the salon to give their nails a buff.
The children shout, 'Yippee, no homework,'
And often drive their mothers berserk.
Fathers get ready for a lot of relaxation
While watching football on the British Broadcasting Corporation.

Georgina Dunham (8)
Katherine Semar Junior School

Spring

S is for spring that comes after wintertime
P is for pressure as newborn lambs try to stand high
R is for running sheep dogs leading from behind
I is for incoming herd of cows on a country lane, moving by
N is for newly grown crops in a line
G is for grooming ponies' coats so fine, and goslings cheeping,
   Be careful, they're behind!

Nicole Crowder (8)
Katherine Semar Junior School

The Unicorn

U is for unicorn, standing proud
N is for nice and gentle
I is for incredible and strong
C is for the colour, pink and purple
O is for over the clouds
R is for rare and beautiful
N is for noble and kind.

Hannah Goode (8)
Katherine Semar Junior School

Football

F is for football which is fantastic
O is for oh no, we scored an own goal!
O is for over the goalie's head, oh no, missed
T is for terrific goals from the halfway line
B is for brilliant goals in the top corner
A is for a good skill
L is for luxury skill round the keeper
L is for a loud crowd, cheering in the background.

Oliver Armstrong (8)
Katherine Semar Junior School

My Dad

My dad is loyal and I think he's funny
But at times he can be very grumpy.
He rode from London to Cambridge on his bike.
I like him kissing me goodnight.
He is sporty and sometimes naughty.
In two years he will be forty!
My dad's nickname is more of a shock,
At work they call him the Silver Fox!

Alice Halls (8)
Katherine Semar Junior School

My Allosaurus

I have an allosaurus, he's really rather sweet
And when I go to sleep he nibbles at my feet.
He likes playing in the garden, but all he wants to do is eat.
My allosaurus is purple with spikes and razor blade teeth.
He's very spotty and can get very mucky,
But one thing for sure, to have him, I'm lucky!

Fawn Doggett (9)
Katherine Semar Junior School

Pilplup

Pilplup is dark and light blue,
She has little yellow feet like a duck.
She's not very fast or slow,
She's very little and cute like a newborn puppy.
She is safe, with a trainer.
She has a little bed,
She is very, very warm, like a cosy person.
She goes to training school,
She is very friendly.

Charlotte Clark (8)
Katherine Semar Junior School

In My Garden

Flowers, glistening over the moonstone river
Silver fish swimming in the pond
Bluebirds flying in the sky

Golden apples hanging on the ruby bush
A chocolate dog, barking at the silver fish
Scarlet leaves on a green tree trunk
Moonstone river, glistening in the sun.

Victoria Peet (7)
Katherine Semar Junior School

In My Magical Place

I have a glittering, pink castle
I have a pet butterfly and a pet dog as well
And the trees are glittering
But snow is crispy
And a sun is shining smoothly in the air
It goes here, there and everywhere
And flowers grow everywhere.

Elicia Draper (7)
Katherine Semar Junior School

Friendship

F is for fun we have together
R is for running free in the summer holidays
I is for icing cakes
E is for friends full of energy
N is for nice friends I have
D is for dancing to music
S is for sunny days and playing in the fields
H is for happy days
I is for ice skating
P is for the school playground we play in.

Chloe Smith (8)
Katherine Semar Junior School

The Sea Of Ice
(Inspired by 'The Sea of Ice' by Caspar David Friedrich)

The jagged teeth, the freezing lips
The sharp hair, the hooked nose
The crumbled eyes with the spiked lashes
The evil face, the powerful ice monster
Strikes again.

Sarah Bevan (9)
Katherine Semar Junior School

The Sea Of Ice
(Inspired by 'The Sea of Ice' by Caspar David Friedrich)

The ice looked evil and huge
The ice caught the boat
And it pulled and pulled
The boat crumbled
Like crisp packets
And it made a racket
It was stuck there
For over 100 years.

Charlotte Hurrell (9)
Katherine Semar Junior School

Adventure Land

The gentle clouds lift you up and down.
The sun's rays are like a heat ray.
There are chocolate walled houses and gates.

Down at the shop you can buy Infinity Wishes
Or buy a Muddle Goblin.
Raining candyfloss falls down,
Because you have a Muddle Goblin.

And you never get fat or thin.
And there's a river of magic milk.

Daniel Hawkins (7)
Katherine Semar Junior School

The Sea Of Ice
(Inspired by 'The Sea of Ice' by Caspar David Friedrich)

Icebergs grab at ships then they're sailing past.
You don't have a chance if your ship's a sailing mast.
Ice is evil, it's Evel Knievel,
You don't want to go near ice!
Imagine it's winter, you're in your car,
If you think about it thoroughly,
You won't go far!

Brody Thomson (9)
Katherine Semar Junior School

The Sea Of Ice
(Inspired by 'The Sea of Ice' by Caspar David Friedrich)

Ice is a devil
It is very evil
Ice is sharp
Ice is like a dagger.

Madison McCandless (9)
Katherine Semar Junior School

The Sea Of Ice
(Inspired by 'The Sea of Ice' by Caspar David Friedrich)

Its razor-sharp claws slicing the wood like it was paper
The teeth as sharp as knives, when one touches something it immediately turns to ice.
For all the fearless people that go out here, none return.
To all the other people, the lucky ones,
That is why all their loved ones end up dead.

Hayley Irwin (9)
Katherine Semar Junior School

The Sea Of Ice
(Inspired by 'The Sea of Ice' by Caspar David Friedrich)

The ice is as pointed as a knife
It was as crumbled as cake
It is scary as a vampire
It is as sharp as a shark's tooth
It was as gooey as an evil monster
It is as vicious as a murderous monster
It was as mean as a wolf
It was as scary as a witch.

Lauren Sumner (9)
Katherine Semar Junior School

My Magical Place

If I ruled the world
I would be a pop girl
And would sing to a crowd
So they would gather round
I would be very happy
And would earn lots of money
And my mum would have some honey.

Ashleigh Monk (7)
Katherine Semar Junior School

The Sea Of Ice
(Inspired by 'The Sea of Ice' by Caspar David Friedrich)

As sharp as a shark's tooth
Looks like a great, big spear
Never go near
It's dangerous

Cold through to the bone
Heavier than a stone
Never go near
It's dangerous

You'll get a chill
Then pay the bill
Never go near
It's dangerous

Blocks of ice
If it hits, twice the price
Never go near
It's dangerous.

Rebecca Sumner (9)
Katherine Semar Junior School

The Sea Of Ice
(Inspired by 'The Sea of Ice' by Caspar David Friedrich)

Ice is fierce
Ice is extensive
Ice is congealed
Ice is pointed
Ice is rock solid
Ice is slippery
Ice is dangerous
Ice is like teeth
Ice is sharp.

Ryan Greenaway (9)
Katherine Semar Junior School

In My Garden You Can See Lots Of Stuff

In my garden you can see creatures,
Birds chirping,
Leaves falling,
Squirrels scampering,
Dogs playing,
Insects scurrying,
Fish swimming calmly,
Furious people, stamping their feet firmly,
Wizards snoring,
Babies crying,
Fire engines flying past,
Aeroplanes soaring past,
Up and down.

Jesse Caldwell (7)
Katherine Semar Junior School

The Sea Of Ice
(Inspired by 'The Sea of Ice' by Caspar David Friedrich)

Painting - The Sea of Ice

The ice is like sharp daggers.
It is frozen solid.
The ship is broken into pieces of wood,
All that is left is a cabin.
It's sinking, deeper and deeper down.
It is a shipwreck.
There is snow everywhere,
The snow is cursed.

Luke Jackson (9)
Katherine Semar Junior School

I Love Everything

Cartwheels, handstands, I do the lot.
When I sing my sister loses the plot.
When I go shopping I buy the whole shop.
I always dance to funky hip hop.
Punch, flick, scissor-kick, karate is my style.
I've only done it for a while.
Front crawl, back crawl, breaststroke, jump, dive.
I love swimming, I love everything!

Rae-lee Coe (9)
Katherine Semar Junior School

In My Magical Place

There are massive flowers, as huge as a house.
The flowers are made from cake.

There are puffy clouds, made from marshmallow.
The sun looks beautiful,
It glows nicely in the day and sleeps under a cloud at night.
The birds sit in the tree tweeting beautifully.

Aimee Savill (7)
Katherine Semar Junior School

The Sea Of Ice

(Inspired by 'The Sea of Ice' by Caspar David Friedrich)

The iced, frosty land
Your fierce crumbled hand.
There will be scary creatures.
When you're saved, you'll have frightened features.

Raj Ranavaya (9)
Katherine Semar Junior School

The Sea Of Ice
(Inspired by 'The Sea of Ice' by Caspar David Friedrich)

I hate ice
Ice is evil
Ice is dangerous
Ice is big
Ice is a giant
Ice is scary
Ice is annoying
Ice is extremely cold
Ice is enormous
Ice means danger.

Sam Lewis (10)
Katherine Semar Junior School

My Fat Pig

My pig is very fat
It got a big smack
My pig is fat,
It's a bit stinky.
My pig lays on its back,
My pig, its name is Pinkey.

My pig is a big disgrace,
He kicks mud onto my face.

Alfie Marks (9)
Katherine Semar Junior School

The Summer's Breeze

The blossom castle is whispering to the breeze
Big, fat bees sitting in the leaves
A massive crowd of leaves shuffling with the breeze
We all like to feel the summer breeze
Birds singing in the trees.

Rowan Osborne (7)
Katherine Semar Junior School

A Magical Garden

In a magic garden there are fantastic golden fish
in an amazing silver pond.
Beautiful bronze cats and dogs
are closest to the moonstone pond.
Purple and gleaming birds are chirping in the trees,
Fantastic green and blue parrots

The moonstone path leads to the sparkling river,
Moonstone frogs in the pond with tadpoles.
Golden apples hanging from silver trees,
Silver pears on a golden bush.

Frogs are drinking water,
Fishes are drinking water too.
There are watersnakes in the other pond.

Jade Hall (7)
Katherine Semar Junior School

The Magic Car

In my magical place
There is a car
That goes fast
It can become a speedboat
The fastest one of all.
There are strawberry birds
That are made of vanilla ice cream
Chocolate clouds in the sky
And the trees are all strong flavours
In the afternoon the sun shines
There are lots of trees and racing cars.

George Bennett (7)
Katherine Semar Junior School

The Lonely Pig

The lonely pig, with no family or friends
He loves his food and drink
Excited to eat away.

Longing for a best friend or just a friend
On a cold winter's day, getting colder each day.
No one to comfort him and keep him warm,
Excited too when summer is coming.
Lonely on a long winter's day.
You just can't imagine what it feels like!

Poor, lonely, unloved pig,
In a horrible, cold stable,
Going to be spring very soon,
The lonely pig is thinking.

Nicole Kemp (9)
Katherine Semar Junior School

The Sea Of Ice
(Inspired by 'The Sea of Ice' by Caspar David Friedrich)

Like clouds in the water,
A snow-white cat, tensed muscles.
Waiting for prey to devour.
As ships come, watch out, you could get pounced.
Sending its claws onto the deck.
Watch out, you could be next!
It's numbing, cold teeth freeze your bones.
Run for the lifeboats, leave it to devour.
Pray it won't see you slip through its claws.

Harriet Dunwoody (9)
Katherine Semar Junior School

Rugby World Cup

Rugby can be hard,
Rugby is pain,
Although it is a good sport.

Sometime I just forget what to do,
My favourite is Leicester,
But I like other teams too.
I don't usually watch rugby,
I'm always in the garden.

Rugby is different to other sport like football.
They pick the ball up in rugby, to score tries.
In football you score goals.
I myself don't play rugby I play football.

I can imagine being tackled by a player,
My dad says that he doesn't understand, nor do I really.
Occasionally I play a game of rugby with my friends.
Rugby is hard, rugby is fun,
I like rugby because you have to run.

Lewis Sell (9)
Katherine Semar Junior School

A Magical Garden

In a fantastic garden
There are golden fish in their silver pond.
Bronze cats and dogs
Are sleeping very near the silver pond.
Green and red birds
Are chirping in the trees.
Perfect pink hamsters
Are having fun.

Patricia Attwood (7)
Katherine Semar Junior School

The Lion

Lions have no fear,
They can very well hear.
They all stalk their prey,
Their prey can only pray.
Lions hunt in prides,
And they have lots of pride.

Hyenas are their only fear,
When they are young or old.
Some old lions have a lot of worry
To load on their backs.

Lions have no fear,
They can very well hear.
They all stalk their prey,
Their prey can only pray.
Lions hunt in prides,
And they have lots of pride.

Joshua Lao (9)
Katherine Semar Junior School

In My Garden

In a beautiful, secret garden,
There are trees, high mountains,
Flowers that never die.
Lovely strawberries that never get out of date.

Bluebirds in this garden, tweeting lovely sounds.
Bunny rabbits, as cute as a smile
And a poor little cat with one eye.
Dogs barking very loud with chocolate eyes.

Liam Arnold (8)
Katherine Semar Junior School

My Older Sister

I have an older sister
But she can get a blister
I do love her very much
She still gobbles up her lunch.

I want her to be perfect
But she's like a circuit
Round and round then work
She's like a spy, search then lurk!

She does help
And she helps dogs if they yelp
But what about me?
Can't she see?
I need love
But all she does is shove!

Well, she sometimes she is nice
She has enough spice.
It's just something about her that's rather mean,
Or maybe she just want to be seen!

Lauma Sarkane (9)
Katherine Semar Junior School

In My Garden

In a green garden, a secret garden,
Lived a lizard with beautiful lashes.
Orange apples, yellow pears, red oranges.
Bats on cars, blossom on houses.
Trees of chocolate and cats laying on rosy rivers.
Ice cream van is here.
Bits for you and me.
Dogs are barking very loud,
With chocolate eyes and golden tails.

Lee Watts (7)
Katherine Semar Junior School

My Imaginary Land

If I ruled the world there would be glowing windows.
Crispy leaves in the sea.
Blossoming trees gently swaying.
Squishy apples make the days.
Big fat bees buzzing around,
And coming out to see the ground.
Flowing bubbles in the fondue.
Chocolate melted on your crunchy lettuce.
In the corn make a fruit salad.
Birds singing in their nests,
Eating worms in their nests.
Dazzling clothes in the shops.
Tides turning the clock.

Chloe Starr (7)
Katherine Semar Junior School

My Monkey

I have a monkey
He is very funky
He has a gorilla friend, he is chunky
He likes to swing about and do his thing
And he likes to wear a diamond ring.

He's very cheeky
and all the animals think he's sneaky.

He wears all different kinds of hats
and scares the rats.
He likes to smile
and look at the businessman's file.

Liam Stalley (9)
Katherine Semar Junior School

My Magical Garden

Trees have blossom and the birds are singing.
Graceful birds flying in the air.
You can hear the children playing in the sun,
Bright, beaming sun, shining on the ground.

Trees that grow chocolate bars
And that have maple syrup inside them.
Magical grass that smells like strawberries.
Chocolate frogs, bouncing around.

Alfie Summers (7)
Katherine Semar Junior School

My Secret Garden

In a garden, a secret garden
Is a beautiful unicorn.
Lots of flowers everywhere,
Growing every day.

In a garden, a secret garden,
Is a rosy river,
And a big, old apple tree.

In a garden, a secret garden
Are little birds singing on the wall,
And little ladybirds flying everywhere.

Danielle Kidd (7)
Katherine Semar Junior School

The Devil

The Devil is a scorching soul
It likes to be as hot as burning coal
The way it dances in the shadows
Also the way it burns down meadows
We also should know that,
Its best friend is a murderous troll.

Eleanor Seager (9)
Katherine Semar Junior School

Golden Squirrels

Golden squirrels rush back and forward, getting acorns.
Little silver birds sing very sweetly in the trees.
Multicoloured flowers grow in the warm sun.
A pure chocolate waterfall,
When it hits the bottom changes into melted mint.
A gingerbread house, made with mint for the windows,
Candy canes for the windowsills,
A Smartie for the doorbell,
Toffee and mint for the roof
And gingerbread for the rest.

Cameron Brown (7)
Katherine Semar Junior School

The Magic Garden

Sparkling snow on the trees, that never melts.
In autumn there are brown bushes that come every year.
Bumblebees that are pink and red.
Dragonflies looping and leaping around your head.

A chocolate waterfall with fish swimming with golden sparks.
Plastic fruit that is extremely edible.
Water that comes out green but is normal.
A tiny house that when you go inside is enormous.

Isabella White (8)
Katherine Semar Junior School

In My Garden

In my garden is a beautiful pond.
In the beautiful pond is a tiny fish.
In my garden sometimes it is under the deep sea.
In my garden sometimes it is in the galaxy.
In my garden there are aliens.

Minh-Nhan Vo (8)
Katherine Semar Junior School

The Boggart

It glides across the sky
Gasps come from passers-by
It swoops down and lands
and turns into a cat,
then a rat

It runs into the street,
Shrieks and screams come from
the crowd behind
nobody had in their mind
that it was harmless
It goes around the corner
and before anyone sees turns into a car,
It zooms away,
It goes into the sea as a killer whale
All the fish say, 'Aren't you pale?'

It keeps changing
until one day
it changes into a snail
and with a wail
it realises it couldn't turn back

It is a shape-shifter
a Boggart without evil
For you see everything
runs out like a battery
the Boggart's power ran out
You can still see it today
as a snail weaving in and out of leaves
leaving a trail behind
a snail trail
It can never die
Endlessly being trodden on

There is a lesson:
Be who you are, don't keep changing
or you will be stuck with what you hate.

Matthew Snares (9)
Katherine Semar Junior School

My Secret Garden

In my garden there are beautiful butterflies, fluttering around.
Apples growing on the apple trees,

Bumblebees coming here and there collecting honey.
Hedgehogs in my flower patch,
And birds eating bread,
And fish in my pond,

Squirrels collecting nuts.
Yellow sunshine in my secret garden.

Zack Perry Brace (8)
Katherine Semar Junior School

In My Garden

I know a wizard garden
Where golden squirrels run to the trees,
Where the sun shines in the sky,
Where flowers are singing in the grass,
Where little ants are walking on the ground,
Where beautiful birds sing in the trees,
Where kids are shouting in the playground,
Where fish are blowing bubbles in the pond,
Where balls are bouncing on the ground.

Korhelia Groralewska (8)
Katherine Semar Junior School

In The Blossoming Trees

Smiley clouds float above chocolate houses.
Talking dogs lay under blossoming trees.
Face paint, trampolines,
Sea coral of different colours,
Blue, black, yellow, white and green.

Jake Van Weede (7)
Katherine Semar Junior School

The Deadly Death Dragon

The deadly death dragon lurks in the deep blue sea.
You better watch out for it may creep and pounce!
If you see its shadow you'd better shout for help.

So beware for it might shoot fire from its wide nostrils
Then you will be toast
and you will look as though you've seen a ghost!

Hide in your bed, for the dragon's very red.
You had better shout *watch out!*

Harley Camp (9)
Katherine Semar Junior School

In My Magical Place

Ice-topped mountains
Fluffy marshmallow clouds,
White mushrooms as tall as mountains.
Cinderella and her prince,
Beautiful butterflies and flowers.
A huge house with high turrets
And a beautiful garden.

Pramita Gurung (7)
Katherine Semar Junior School

The Match

F un, fast and keeps you fit
O pen goal
O wen scoring every match
T eams and tackles
B oot the ball into goal
A lan Shearer's hat-trick
L ong kick up the pitch
L ast second goes - *goal!*

Bailey Ridlington (9)
Katherine Semar Junior School

My Magic City

The crunchy clouds made of dooming sweets,
That make your nose twist again.
A dazzling rainbow, where a magnificent queen sleeps.
The fizziest, busiest Coca-Cola building that blasts joy.
A tasty candyfloss building that shouts, *'Eat me!'*
So every day the people come and eat me like never before,
And you never get caught and your teeth don't rot.

Julia Belteki (7)
Katherine Semar Junior School

My Chelsea Team

If I made the world
It would be a gigantic stadium,
With chocolate goals at each end.
The crowd would cheer my name as I arrived.
As I am the greatest footballer.
I would score 100 goals.
Chelsea would call me up
And England would be my goal.

Mason McCandless (8)
Katherine Semar Junior School

Trick Or Treat

H is for Hallowe'en it's fun
A is for a costume that your wear
L is for a little bit scared
L is for being lonely
O is for only having fun
W is for wicked ghosts on the run
E is for being excited at Hallowe'en
E is for everyone going trick or treating
N is for Hallowe'en is nearly here.

Ashleigh-Jo Hare (9)
Katherine Semar Junior School

The Magical Band

Everybody is playing, everything is new
Everybody will play with you.
There is a scrunchie mountain which pours chocolate.
Everybody is kind and sharing.
Lots of wonderful people, not bullying, they're caring.
There are lots of bands and the glossy crowd love it.
But most of all everybody likes the drum kit.
Then a two-headed bulldog comes into the room,
And everybody tries to touch it,
But then it goes zoom.
Everybody gets back to the band,
The children clutching their mother's hand.

Tom Seager (7)
Katherine Semar Junior School

My Imaginary Land

Ice cone mountains on the ground,
There are lots of these, all around.
Flying fish in the air,
Then they see a bubbling bear.
Chocolate rivers and waterfalls,
Children playing on the walls.
Glossy flowers flowing here and there,
Crispy leaves everywhere.
Beaming sunshine, shining down,
No one in this world has a frown.
Dinky doodles in the book,
Glowing fingers have a look.

Olivia Alltree (8)
Katherine Semar Junior School

The Most Magical Place Ever

There is an ice cream fountain,
That bubbles and flows.
The golden flowers ring and sing
And the whispering trees blow.

The sun is made of marshmallows,
Which float to the ground.
The castle sits upon a hill,
Underneath a windmill.

A winding stream through the valley,
Chocolate ducks quacking really loudly.
The hairy dog walking over the narrow bridge.

Joshua Weeks (7)
Katherine Semar Junior School

The Haunted Traffic Light

Traffic light, traffic light gives you a fright,
Traffic light, traffic light gives all his might,
Traffic light, traffic light beam your light,
Traffic light, traffic light can't fly a kite,
Traffic light, traffic light isn't afraid of heights!
Traffic light, traffic light stands like a soldier,
Traffic light, traffic light gets much colder,
Traffic light, traffic light gets much older
Traffic light, traffic light he will be immortal!

Jonah Alltree (9)
Katherine Semar Junior School

Hallowe'en

Everyone, it's Hallowe'en
Dress up in costumes, sing and scream
People give out sweets and cake
Which they take time to cook and make
We put out pumpkins to scare everyone
When we get frightened we've got to run
All the houses are pretty scary
We even might dress as Bloody Mary
It's very dark when we walk outside
The outdoor world is pretty wide
But at least we have lots of fun
And eat all the candy we all won
Hallowe'en is better than anything
Even parents are allowed to join in
And eat all the candy they all win
Everyone, it's Hallowe'en
Dress up in costumes, sing and scream.

Tia Burrett (9)
Katherine Semar Junior School

Hallowe'en Fright At Night

H appy to be trick or treating
A nd the dead people come alive
L ovely costumes to wear
L ots of graveyards
O ut in the night trick or treating
W itches flying about
E vil spirits lark around
E veryone getting sweets
N asty ghosts hiding.

Oakleigh-Anne Brace (9)
Katherine Semar Junior School

My Magical Place

A hairy dog with ice cream legs,
Creeping caterpillars with tongues as long as a school,
Looking for some metal flies to munch on.
Gigantic flowers with tinkly bells.
A purple merman with poisonous spikes.
Candy sun with ice cream mash.
A chocolate milkshake pond with cream on top.

The drawbridge becomes invisible and moves up,
Invisible carriages go clunk, clunk, clunk.

James Bovaird (7)
Katherine Semar Junior School

My Pet

My panda has lots of hair
You may think it's very rare.
People in the street stare,
I think it's unfair,
Just because my panda has hair!

My panda's rather funky,
You should see him when he's hunky!
People say he's lazy
But I just say he's crazy!

My panda is black and white,
Sometimes he's in a fight,
But I don't mind, he's alright!

Rachel Holland (9)
Katherine Semar Junior School

The Dragon

T he dragon was scary
H e had bad breath
E xcited to eat.

D ragon's teeth are sharp
R ough scales
A ny dragon is big
G ordon is his name
O n his fiery bed
N obody can defeat him.

T J Baker (10)
Katherine Semar Junior School

England FC

England are the best,
The birds are building a nest,
Ready for the football match,
Everyone's getting out the window hatch.

England rule,
The stands are full,
For the match in Hull.

England kick off,
And they score,
Then they hear a roar
From the huge crowd.

Daniel Weeks (9)
Katherine Semar Junior School

Hallowe'en

H allowe'en is fun
A nd scary costumes
L ovely, scary night
L ots of monsters running about
O ne scary night
W e all like having fun
E veryone likes Hallowe'en
E veryone goes in scary costumes
N ice, scary night.

Nikita Schooling (9)
Katherine Semar Junior School

Fireworks

Fireworks shimmer
Fireworks bright
Fireworks dazzle
Day and night
Fireworks sizzle
Fireworks shine
Fireworks glimmer
All get in line
Look at all the colours
Up in the air
Look how beautiful they are
Everyone will stare.

Lauren Starr (9)
Katherine Semar Junior School

Football

Football is fun
And played in the sun
It's Arsenal vs Man United,
And the crowd is very excited..

Arsenal scored a goal
But it hit the post.
It was half-time
And that was fine.

It was a goal kick
But he slipped on a stick
Man U scored a goal
And it was one-one

It was full time
And the score was one-one.
They all had a bun
And that was fun.

After the match
They all had a party.
At the party they shook hands
With all the fans.

Joshua Broughall (9)
Katherine Semar Junior School

Life Is Great

Life is great, life is wonderful
Sometimes life can be a handful!
Everyone enjoys life, it's cool.
In summer people get out a pool!
Life is sometimes tough
And it is sometimes rough!
I enjoy life
And I'm sure you do too.

Rachael Sumner (9)
Katherine Semar Junior School

World War 101

There was a place,
Called Kumbajum,
Which is a place
Where they all drink rum.
They were all hurt
And some were dying,
The humans were winning,
The chips were frying.
Mojo had the bling,
Keskrin could sing.
Mojo swallowed an onion ring,
When he went to Burger King.
The humans have won,
On Kumbajum,
But Mojo was still there,
But he wouldn't dare.
Mojo was a terminator,
Not! *More like a Burgernater!*

Billy Thomas (9)
La Salette Catholic Primary School

Calm, Calm Sea

Fishes, sharks, other creatures
Under the sea, on the coral.
The sharks with their features
That are not as beautiful as the Caribbean Ocean.
The roar of the waves you can hear from a mile away.

Calm, calm sea,
And the moonlight reflecting off the waves,
To make the fish come back another day.
Sharks soaring and swaying in the sea, waiting for me.

Taylor Cranshaw (10)
Montgomerie Junior School

Snowy, Snowy Evening

Snowy, snowy evening,
Here I stand watching the snow drift slowly,
like a big, white sheet,
hearing the birds tweeting happily.

Snowy, snowy evening,
taste the cold snowflakes on my tongue,
smell the soup, quickly boiling on the stove,
And feeling wet snow melting in my hands.

Snowy, snowy evening,
Time for bed.
The next day arrives, the sun comes out,
no more snow drifting,
no birds tweeting,
no more soup in my tum,
and no more snow this winter again.

Caitlin Dellar (8)
Montgomerie Junior School

Snowy, Snowy Night

Snowy, snowy night,
Here I stand, snow drifting flurries,
Catch the silver thatch,
As cold as an ice pole.

Snowy, snowy night,
Then it falls heavily,
Then softly it calmed.
Another year we wait again,
To have some snow to sing about.

Snowy, snowy night,
As soft as cotton wool,
Floating, drifting, falling now.

Tristan Lewis (8)
Montgomerie Junior School

Calm, Calm Sea

Calm, calm, calm sea
The sea rises
Up to the skies
The water flows
The water glows.

Calm, calm, calm sea
The sea is swirling
The sea is twirling
The sea is rough
The fish go puff.

Calm, calm, calm sea
I see the moon
The fireworks go boom
The sun is gone to bed
Now it's time for me to rest my head.

Amy Sparrow (9)
Montgomerie Junior School

Sunny, Sunny Beach

Sunny, sunny beach
People shouting
People running
People tormenting seagulls

Sunny, sunny beach
Smell of ice cream
Smell of chips
Smell of salty water

Sunny, sunny beach
I see the sea
I see the sand
I see the seagulls.

Tate Royer (9)
Montgomerie Junior School

A Snowy, Snowy Night

A snowy, snowy night,
I am sitting down in the warmth,
Watching the snow falling down so light,
As I smell the roast being cooked.

A snowy, snowy night,
The chair I'm sitting on is as soft as silk,
Watching through the window with only snow in sight,
I can only hear the sound of the TV.

A snowy, snowy night,
I see the snow drifting from the sky,
The hotel is an amazing height,
I watch the sea rising up.

A snowy, snowy night,
The snow is as white as paper,
I suddenly see people having a snowball fight,
There's a pond covered with thick ice.

Shannon Goodwin (10)
Montgomerie Junior School

The Hot, Sunny Sunset

The hot, sunny sunset
I hear the calm sea.
My feet sink into soft, cool sand,
I feel peaceful.

The hot, red sunset,
Not a cloud in sight.
Water rises and tickles my toes,
I feel peaceful.

Connor Tyler (9)
Montgomerie Junior School

The Sunny, Sunny Zoo

At the sunny, sunny zoo
There are lions and penguins and cheetahs too
There are giraffes and elephants and hyenas, more
And the monkeys go *oh oh, ah ah.*

At the sunny, sunny zoo
All the cows go moo, moo, moo
The sheep go baa, baa, baa
I can see the animals all so big
There are seals and rhinos and meerkats too
I can see a monkey and it looks like you.

At the sunny, sunny zoo
I can smell the animals and their food
I can eat the ice cream and it tastes so good
Some of the cages are made out of wood
Monkey escapes, give it a smack
Teat time, got to go, gotta pack!

Rosie Webster (9)
Montgomerie Junior School

It's A Snowy, Snowy Day

It's a snowy, snowy day
Time to shout, hip hip hooray
Now is the time for a snowball fight
The snow is so white.

It's a snowy, snowy day
Let's go outside and play
Let's make a snowman
Now it's the end of the day.

Snowy, snowy day
End of the day.

Britney Lashmar (10)
Montgomerie Junior School

A Stormy, Stormy Day

Stormy, stormy, stormy day
Trees dripping, forests flooding.
People going, ponds growing.

Stormy, stormy, stormy day,
Lakes flourishing, houses demolishing,
Forests disappearing, people arguing.

Stormy, stormy, stormy day,
Hailstones falling, animals drowning,
People running, rats swimming.

Stormy, stormy, stormy day,
People drowning, people moving,
Rain falling, electricity failing,
It's a stormy, stormy day.

Alex Pate (9)
Montgomerie Junior School

Snowy Day

One snowy, snowy, snowy day
I went outside and it was very snowy.
Me and my mates were being very funny.
It was snowing outside.

One snowy, snowy, snowy day,
I was making a snowman,
It was really fun.

One snowy, snowy, snowy day,
I skidded across the crunchy ice,
Crisp, crisp, crisp as my feet
Went across the ice,
And I saw a white, white, white snowy day.

William Taylor (9)
Montgomerie Junior School

The Grassy, Grassy Field

Once in a dark field a man was walking through the field.
He was walking through the grass and then he found a bit of brass,
The brass was a bronze bowl.

The grassy, grassy field, he picked up the brass
And kept on walking,
And after that he found a very sharp piece of glass.

The grassy, grassy field,
Meanwhile you could see some trees in the distance,
Crickets chirping,
You could see the river flowing and the frogs croaking.

The grassy, grassy field,
Trees tall, river long
Anything else would be so good.

Christopher Whitlock (9)
Montgomerie Junior School

Calm, Calm Sea

Calm, calm sea,
Creatures are swimming to their homes,
The water is drifting out,
The seabed is going down.

Calm, calm sea,
I see people's boats slowing down,
I smell the coldness of ice cream,
I hear seagulls' *'ark'* noises.

Calm, calm sea,
I can feel the air blowing around me,
I can taste the warm hot dogs,
I can touch the sandy sand, falling out of my hands.

Shannon Townsend (9)
Montgomerie Junior School

Calm Sea

Calm sea, sun going down
The fish are going to bed
And swimming around.

Calm sea, I can see the sea
I can hear the sounds of the sea
I can taste the salty sea,
I can touch the boat.

Calm sea, in the boat,
We are swaying side to side
It made me a bit sick.

Calm sea,
We are swaying very quickly in the boat
Because the waves are going to roar.

Samantha Doe (8)
Montgomerie Junior School

The Snowy Winter's Day

A snowy, snowy, snowy day
I lie beneath the drifting sky
And am laying on the crystal snow.

A snowy, snowy, snowy day
I see people having snowballs fights
And no adults in the children's sights
And no children playing with kites.

A snowy, snowy, snowy day
The cold is breezy and now I'm getting a little bit wheezy,
Now I'm getting really sneezy!

Michelle Sillitoe (8)
Montgomerie Junior School

A Windy Day

A windy day is today
With birds singing everywhere
Clouds drifting, kites swinging,
Also planes flying all ways.

A windy day is today,
Kids running, waves big,
On the wind it rises with power
And tornadoes are forming.

A windy day is today,
The wind is swishy, loud like thunder,
I wish it would last forever.

A windy day is today.

Morgan Davies (8)
Montgomerie Junior School

The Dark, Dark Ocean

On the dark, dark ocean bed
I lie beneath the coral reefs,
Rainbow fish swim above my head,
It's too quiet, I'm a little bit scared.

On the dark, dark ocean bed,
No sharks to be seen, just you and me,
Swimming across the sea,
Bubbles, bubbles surrounding me,
And my Nintendo Wii.

Keeley Pitt-Stanley (9)
Montgomerie Junior School

Summer's, Summer's Day

Summer's, summer's day
People swimming in the sea,
Playing in the sand,
Eating yummy ice creams,
On boiling hot land.

Summer's, summer's day
Feel the sand as soft as flour,
Seagulls flying high,
Smell the salty water,
On the sunbeds you can lie.

Summer's, summer's day
Feel the warm breeze,
Rushing through your hair,
People making sandcastles,
In the bursting air.

Summer's, summer's day
Children being noisy,
Shouting more and more,
Waves that rise up so gently
Then crash down on the shore.

Summer's, summer's day
The blazing, hot sun
Shining on your hair,
See the boats bob,
Little birds here and there.

Summer's, summer's day
Touch the silky sand,
Splashing in the sea,
Getting really sandy,
Playing happily.

Alice Lawrence (8)
Montgomerie Junior School

Misty, Misty Night

Misty, misty night
Drifting across the black, crispy clouds
As I watch
It tastes like deep coldness.

Misty, misty night
Sparkling cobwebs
Silvery, damp grass
And trees.

Luke Rock (9)
Montgomerie Junior School

Sunny Day

Ocean water
Calm and blue
Ocean water
Sparkling too

Small boats
Big floats
Bobbing along
Going ding dong

Blazing sunshine
Drinking white wine
Sandy morning
Baby's crawling

People calling
Bird poop falling
Children swimming
Children swinging

Balloons popping
Children stopping
Shark attack
Time to pack.

Elle MacDonald (8)
Montgomerie Junior School

The Old Moon

The rusty old thing has no gravity, has no air
Bounce to bounce, flying to buy stuff for the trip

The old rusty thing is cold, a silent planet
Quiet everywhere, a misty sight, quiet as a mouse
Dead as a field, alone without anybody else
It is as peaceful as Earth

This is such fun, no gravity
From front-flip to back-flip to side-flip
To fun jumping, this is such a great planet
It is fun to float, swiftly jumping on the planet
Spinning on this planet

Wow! I think this planet is great
I just take my last floaty steps on the rusty old planet
I float back to my rocket
On Earth I take a last look at the moon.

Patrick Mackinnon (8)
Montgomerie Junior School

Misty, Misty Night

A dark, gloopy mist hit the air,
Grey and cold it fell heavily below,
It covered the village silently.

Misty, misty night,
Villagers angrily shout,
'Where is the sun?'

Misty, misty night,
Out came the sun,
Hip hip hooray!

Iona Shaw (9)
Montgomerie Junior School

Snowy, Snowy Night

Snowy, snowy morning
When the children wake
They get on the clothes and gloves
Get outside, make a snowman.

Snowy, snowy morning
When the white, cold, silver snow flies by
It's melting at noon, it's slush at night,
Slippery soft, as cold as a freezer.

Snowy, snowy night
Floating gently, hits the ground
Seeing the lakes freeze
Melting slowly, almost gone.

Joshua Wiggins (9)
Montgomerie Junior School

Snowy, Snowy Day

Snowy, snowy day,
Ice-cold snow,
And the bare trees.

Snowy, snowy day,
The silver moon
That shines that silver light.

Snowy, snowy day,
Snow gently falling down
Through the day.

Snowy, snowy day,
Kids playing through the day,
What a great, snowy day!

Megan White (9)
Montgomerie Junior School

Snowy, Snowy Day

Snowy, snowy day
Here I stand
Soft, slippery, silver snow,
Pretty snowflakes falling silently
From the sky.

Snowy, snowy day
Children making snow angels in the
Soft, slippery snow,
Adults can't drive
Because of the silver, wet snow.

Snowy, snowy day
Children making snow angels
And snowmen
And gliding across the ice.

Snowy, snowy day
Frosted trees,
On Christmas Eve,
We will get presents to receive,
Snowy, snowy day.

Elise Winning (8)
Montgomerie Junior School

Sunny, Sunny Afternoon

Sunny, sunny afternoon
As we happily go to the beach,
Crashing waves, as hot as the moon,
Ice cream's melting, children screaming.

Sunny, sunny afternoon
Burning, weaving sand children play in,
Ice cream man ringing his bell,
Children screaming at their mums.

Sunny, sunny afternoon
As we sweat from the heat,
Children playing catch and throw.

Sunny, sunny afternoon
Children splashing in the waves,
Baking sun children stand under
In their towels.

Sunny, sunny afternoon
As they head home to their beds,
Children sleeping, *zzzz,*
All sound asleep.

Hannah Broad (8)
Montgomerie Junior School

Winter, Winter Day

Winter, winter day
Silver, cold weather,
Drifting down the bright trees
Kids building snowmen,
Sticks, stones, carrot nose.

Winter, winter day
Fresh air, gold light,
Snow zigzagging
Down a tree,
Snow angels on the ground,
It doesn't make a sound.

Winter, winter day
Taste snowflakes
From the sky,
In winter birds don't fly.

Winter, winter day
Stomp, stomp, snow ruffling
Down the street all kids,
Messing around,
With their snowy, snowy feet.

Chloe Larkins (9)
Montgomerie Junior School

Calm Sea

Waiting by the calm sea,
Lauren, Sam and me.
Babies paddle in the stream,
Little kids eating ice cream.

Daddy's shouting, 'Come here,'
Family's walking up the pier,
Little dogs having a roar,
Family's taking the tour.

Mummy's reading a big book,
Go to the shop, just have a look.
Kids wearing water wings,
Everyone's eating Burger Kings.

Nana's drinking a glass of beer,
The biggest boat, let's scream and cheer!
Conga game flies and bedtime comes,
Time to get called by our mums.

When home switch off the light,
Time to say *night-night!*

Beth Healey (8)
Montgomerie Junior School

Snowy, Snowy, Day

Snowy, snowy day,
Children playing in the snow,
Drifting, melting snow,
Children making snow angels.

Snowy, snowy day,
Smell of hot chocolate,
Children playing snowmen,
People walking in the crunchy snow,
Hot chocolate dripping in my mouth.

Snowy, snowy day
Melting snow as it drifts on cars,
Swooping, swaying arms and legs,
While children make snow angels.

Snowy, snowy day,
Silently, slowly, quietly and carefully,
Children going to their homes,
Calmly they shut the door.

Snow coming through my gloves
When I build a snowman.
Children skidding and hiding in a bush,
They never want the fun to end.

Claudia Claydon (9)
Montgomerie Junior School

Rainy, Rainy Day

Rainy, rainy day,
Everybody looking high
At the downfall of rain
Up in the sky.
Everyone getting wet,
Someone was trying to use a net.

Rainy, rainy day,
Everybody running in water.
Dots flying.
Everything calming down
And then blue skies
Above the town.

Rainy, rainy day,
The downfall started again.
Someone was trying to get to cover,
Then it turned blue again
And everyone was happy now.

Aaron Cole (9)
Montgomerie Junior School

Summer, Summer Day

It's a good, hot day
I smell fish being sold,
I hear seagulls squawking in the air
I see people having fun in the sea
I taste soft, smooth ice cream in my mouth.

Anya Tobin (9)
Montgomerie Junior School

Foggy, Foggy Night

Foggy, foggy night,
The clouds have lost their way,
It's dark and quiet, the stars are anxious,
The moon is shining in the fog.

Foggy, foggy night,
The moon is trying to find the clouds,
The moon is zooming, the stars are swaying,
But the clouds cannot be found.

Foggy, foggy night,
It's nearly morning, there's no more time,
The sun is coming, no just wait,
The sun has come, it's too late.

Maddy McDonald (9)
Montgomerie Junior School

Snowy, Snowy Day

Snowy, snowy day
Snow falling across the bay
Everybody has to pay
People are going to lay

Snowy, snowy day
Everybody playing with snow
Girls putting on the bows
People washing their smelly toes

Snowy, snowy day
Swirling silver, just like snow
People making things with dough
It's the end of the day, time to go.

Jodie Chong (8)
Montgomerie Junior School

Starry, Starry Night

Starry, starry night is very bright
You would never believe the wonderful sight
With the wells and swells in the sky
As you listen to the people cry

Starry, starry night, sky is very tight
All the clouds are at a magnificent height
As the clouds ski the land
As they sweep the sand

Starry, starry night, have you ever seen the tree brown?
Have you ever seen the smokey town?
Have you ever seen the wonderful moon?
Have you ever seen the Egyptian tomb?

Joe Coster (9)
Montgomerie Junior School

Snowy, Snowy Day

Snowy, snowy day
The horses are eating hay
The bells on Santa's sleigh
Are jingling.

Snowy, snowy day
The snow is driving to the ground
Kids are giving each other pounds.

Snowy, snowy day
The day is dawning
The kids are yawning
The kids run down the stairs to open their presents.

Bethany McCreath (8)
Montgomerie Junior School

Snowy, Snowy Day

Snowy, snowy day
Here I am watching the snow drift,
People making snowmen,
I am as cold as can be.

Snowy, snowy day,
The coldness when I pick up some snow,
When I have some snow and it melts,
I can see people having so much fun.

Snowy, snowy day,
The snow feels so cold,
People throwing snowballs,
The day has nearly ended,
Snowy day, you've melted away.

Ross Beckett (8)
Montgomerie Junior School

Snowy, Snowy Night

Snowy, snowy night,
Lots of joy in the town,
Billions beams of light,
Ground's slippery.

Snowy, snowy night,
People playing in the silver snow,
People skiing, going out of sight,
Fantastic lights in the city.

Snowy, snowy night,
Lots of snow falling from the sky,
Raising unbelievable height,
Everybody had a jolly good Christmas.

Harry Fortt (8)
Montgomerie Junior School

Snowy, Snowy Night

Snowy, snowy night,
Gently falling from the sky,
Making a silvery, glittery scene,
Swaying gently to the floor.

Snowy, snowy night,
Glassy icicles clutching icy roofs.
People looking out the window,
Glad they're not out there.

Snowy, snowy night,
Has now turned to early morning.

Jessica Dunmow (9)
Montgomerie Junior School

Snowy, Snowy Night

Snowy, snowy night,
Snow is as cold as ice,
You can touch it, you can taste it,
You can see it flow from the sky.

Snowy, snowy night,
Covering the cars,
Blocking you in,
An ever-changing silent story.

Snowy, snowy night,
Feeling soft and crunchy,
Just like popcorn
Under your feet.

Lilac Limacher (9)
Montgomerie Junior School

Summer, Summer's Day

Summer, summer's day
Sunrays shining on the bay
On the beach people lay
The sun is like a boiling ray
The sky's not grey.

Summer, summer's day
Eating ice cream is not wrong
Children making a lovely song
People watching the film King Kong
Doors making the sound, ding dong.

Summer, summer's day
You can almost smell the salty sea
Everybody looking at me
Kids going down slides, shouting *wee hee*
Children running from the bees.

Bradley Fuller (9)
Montgomerie Junior School

Dark, Dark Night

Dark, dark night
The moon tries to break through,
While the stars glow,
Drifted gently against the sky.

Dark, dark night,
It smells like a storm is coming near,
Animals are crawling around
Looking for cover and food.

Dark, dark night,
Reach out to touch it,
Your hand disappears
In front of your eyes.

Sidnie Wayman (9)
Montgomerie Junior School

Stormy, Stormy Night

Stormy, stormy night
Windows clanging
Gives me a fright
Doors slamming
Stormy, stormy night
Trees screaming
Moon shines white
People weeping.

Ben Goringe (10)
Montgomerie Junior School

The Sly Fox And The Red Hen

Once upon a time there was a little red hen,
she lived on her own in a little wooden den.
One day she went out to collect sticks,
she might even find some berries to pick.
Not far away lived a sly young fox,
he is very poor so he lives in a box.
The fox went out and spotted the hen,
he crept inside her little wooden den.
The fox heard the hen tiptoeing back,
then the fox opened his potato sack.
The fox threw the hen into the bag,
little did he know his coat had an itchy price tag.
So he scratched and he scratched,
as the hen crawled out of the sack.
She filled the sack with heavy rocks,
when the fox got home he slammed them in the pot.
The hot water splashed and killed the fox and his den,
'Ha ha ha,' chuckled the hen.
Then the farmer came and chopped off her head,
as quick as a flash the hen was dead.
No one lived happily ever after,
except the farmer who was bursting with laughter.

Amy Cannell (9)
Nazeing County Primary School

The Three Little Pigs

The three little pigs were bored one day, hot and tired not wanting
to play,
'I want a bargain,' said Tiddlywink, 'I'll buy some hay that's what
I think,'
'I will build a house away from home, I will eat my dinner on my own.'
'I need a door and blue windows too; I need a kitchen and a loo.'
'There is something that worries me, I just don't know,
What if Mr Wolf comes to blow he'll eat me up in one big go,
I'll be in his belly, I'll be dead and rather smelly.'
'Please don't worry I will use *kapow,* anyway I want my house now.'
He built his house in five minutes sharp and cooked his dinner,
fresh fried carp.
But something big and something bad, the wolf came big and glad.
'Hello little pig I'm called Mo,' and he ate the pig in one big go.
Now let's move on to pig number two, this is what he decided to do.
He wanted a house of big brown sticks, he wanted it big so cement
he would mix.
He placed the sticks one to ten. When it was done it looked
like a den.
But again the wolf came and ruined curly tail's art. He killed the pig
with his little son Bart.
Last but not least the porky one, wanted to have a bit of fun.
His two little brothers were vain and dumb; this little piggy was
the clever one.
He got some sticks, only joking bricks!
He built it fine and so divine. But again the wolf came, and he did
his work,
He blew and he blew but soon he learnt. 'I'll go through the chimney
and the dirt.'
In he fell into a pot, and that pot was very hot.
The wolf went red but soon he was dead.
The pink little piggy smiled with care, 'Don't worry little brothers in
Heaven you'll be fine there.'

Nicole Ciccarelli (9)
Nazeing County Primary School

Autumn Poem

Brown, gold, now not green,
Making people very keen,
To go conker hunting all night long,
Whilst singing a little song.

Autumn, autumn, here comes autumn!

Animals beginning to hibernate,
For the long and cold winter state.
Hedgehogs, tortoises, frogs too,
Sleeping warmly beneath you.

Autumn, autumn, here comes autumn!

Leaves scattered everywhere,
Falling, falling here and there.
Acorns sprinkled on the floor,
For squirrels to collect for their winter store.

Autumn, autumn, here comes autumn!

Splashing, kicking in the leaves,
Amongst the webs the spider weaves.
Feeling colder day by day,
No more fields of corn and hay.

Autumn, autumn, here is autumn!
Summer is gone now autumn is here!

Jordan Dennis (10)
Perryfields Junior School

My Autumn Poem

Pack up your summer clothes
And get ready for the autumn.
Autumn days when the grass is jewelled
And the leaves are falling from the trees.
The animals will hide as the air gets cold,
So enjoy the autumn and enjoy the things you have.

Liam Mears
Perryfields Junior School

The Cat

The ginger cat has soft fur,
But comes home covered in burrs.
He is extremely fluffy
But also very cuddly.
He is quite small
And likes to play with a ball.
When he looks at you he is so cute,
He sniffs around the smelly boot.
Now he is playing with my sock
Also he likes sleeping quite a lot.
He is clean and eats runner beans.
He is chasing a twig,
But also chases the pigs.
He is very loud with one big *miaow*.
He sleeps in a basket and he loves it.
He is hunting a mouse in the big farmhouse
And most of all he is lovely and beautiful.

Kianna Offord Pickering (8)
Perryfields Junior School

Autumn Is . . .

Autumn is when leaves fall off the trees,
With all different colours orange, red and brown,
Which glint in the sunlight as they go down, down, down,
While the branches are left to sway in the breeze.

The nights get darker one by one,
It's much darker than before,
The nights will begin by about four,
This all proves autumn has begun.

Emily Wood (10)
Perryfields Junior School

Autumn

Leaves on the trees are falling
Autumn is here again
Squirrels are gathering their food for winter
Autumn is here again
Cold foggy mornings wisp through the trees
Autumn is here again
Until the sun breaks through and warms the ground
Autumn is here again
Harvest time is approaching fast
Autumn is here again
Turn the clock back as the nights are drawing in
Autumn is here again.

Eilish Pudney (10)
Perryfields Junior School

Autumn Is Here

Autumn is finally here,
Summer has come to an end,

Winter is just round the corner,
Crunchy leaves,
Orange, gold and red.

Autumn is here.

Conkers are falling,
Leaves are turning gold and old,

Falling to the ground,
Colours very bold.

Tom Nash (11)
Perryfields Junior School

It's Autumn Time

It's autumn time

In the autumn when the trees are brown
See the pretty leaves falling down,
Hear the wind whistling through the ground

It's autumn time

Hear the leaves crunching on the ground
Orange, yellow, red and brown
See the leaves twisting and turning in the sky
Colours of the leaves gleaming in the sun

It's autumn time.

Elisha Bedding (11)
Perryfields Junior School

Friendship

F riendship, it's like a butterfly gracefully flying
R ough patches along the way
I gnoring with the others
E nding in arguments
N o one to tell whose fault it was
D oing nothing, it's like a
S hip with no water to float on
H ills with no bumps
I gloos with no ice
P eople with a friend.

Alexandra Claire Simmons (11)
Perryfields Junior School

My Poem

Look at the dog,
he is very soft,
but he doesn't like to have a wash.

He is very cuddly,
but sometimes he is muddly.

The dog is very nice,
but he is scared of mice.
The dog is also scared of a frog,
but the frog is not scared of the dog.

The dog is very loud,
but he doesn't miaow.
My dog loves running,
but he doesn't like coming.

Megan Lea (9)
Perryfields Junior School

Football

F ootball is my favourite sport
O n the pitch it's cold
O n the pitch it's muddy
T he referee blows his whistle
B ecause the game begins
A ll the players running around
L ots of tackling, lots of goals
L osers get a cheer as well as winners.

Ryan Shayler (11)
Perryfields Junior School

My Pet Frank

My pet Frank is very nice
But he likes to bring in mice.
He likes to eat a lot of food
And he is mostly in a very good mood.
Frank's fur is black and white
But he does not like to get into fights.
He likes to dance when the music starts
Me and him can never be apart.
He gets on with the other cat
But at least he is not very fat.
Me and Mum we fight over him
We just wish he had a twin.
He is really very fond
Of grabbing a fish out of the pond.
But he does not like to bite,
He prowls around in the dark night.

Millie Austin-Coskry (8)
Perryfields Junior School

My Autumn Poem

A utumn, autumn, it's all around us,
  conkers in the park and leaves on the car.
U mbrellas come down from the attic for the rainy days.
T he conker fights in the playground, shield your eyes!
U nusual leaf colours; try to collect the rainbow of leaves
M any times in autumn are cold but are very enjoyable.
N ow that autumn has gone it's now winter,
  umbrellas go back in the attic and woolly hats come down
  and are put on.

Luke Clarke (10)
Perryfields Junior School

Untitled

There was an old lady
Who lived in a shoe,
With her dog called Boo.
She had so many horses,
She did not know what to do.

While she cleaned out the stables,
She had an idea,
Of laying forty tables,
Covered in horse leg stew.

She cut and cooked them
And made a smelly old brew,
She had so much stew,
She didn't know what to do.

She covered her tables
And made it into fables,
As a strange shop lady
With a dog called Boo.

Samuel Ellingford-Frost (11)
Perryfields Junior School

Autumn Time

Leaves are falling off the trees,
Autumn time is here.
Cold and rainy all day long,
Autumn time is here.
Auburn, red and golden leaves,
Autumn time is here.
Time to sit near the fire,
Autumn time is here!

Tyler Hadlow (11)
Perryfields Junior School

My Sandwich

A fat slice of bread
and a lump of jam,
a chunk of cucumber
and a piece of ham.

A bit of jelly
and a slice of cake,
a Yorkshire pudding
and some pasta bake.

A splash of mayonnaise
and a squirt of pickle,
half a tomato
only costing a nickel!

A peeled potato
and a fat juicy plum,
a portion of lettuce
to give to my chum.

The finishing touch is
an apple tart,
it looks so tasty
but where to start?

Georgina Ginnaw (10)
Perryfields Junior School

My Fish!

Goldie, Goldie orange and white
Goldie, Goldie shining bright
Goldie, Goldie having a fight
Goldie, Goldie when you are gone
Goldie, Goldie makes me happy
Goldie, Goldie holding you tight in my mind!

Charlotte Ginnaw (8)
Perryfields Junior School

Autumn Time

A utumn time is here, so quickly.
U nderwear; extra pants and vests and socks.
T imes of bitter cold and crunching, crackling leaves.
U nderneath our feet the frozen ground
M igrating, swallows, geese and other friends.
N ight-time comes too soon

T rick or treaters knocking on your knocker.
I t is time to resist the frozen bitter cold.
M ilder leaves scattered upon the frosty ground.
E verlasting darkness, so peaceful and calm.

Eric Austin-Coskry (10)
Perryfields Junior School

London Underground

Streaks of metal whizzing past me,
Hear wheels clatter past,
Faulty lighting flickering fast,
Get on train and now you are free.

Train is zooming into station,
Hear it humming with elation,
See kids boarding it with their friends,
The excitement never ends.

Empty train sneaking into siding,
Driver climbs out to have his tea,
Child walks along, parent guiding,
His mouth is grinning with glee.

Daniel Owens (10)
Perryfields Junior School

Little Monsters (Sisters)

Little sisters here they come!
Shooting guns and ruining fun,
Causing paths of destruction,
Little sisters here they come!

Little sisters here they come!
Over mountains and through seas,
Hunting down those little beasts,
Little sisters here they come!

Little sisters here they come!
Towering giants, bossy boots,
Throwing wobblies (bad moods),
Little sisters here they come!

Little sisters here they come!
These little pests do none for the best,
Little groups of invading soldiers,
Little sisters here they come.

Little sisters here they come!
Giving you a very sore tum,
Thinking a plan as sly as a fox,
Little sisters here they come!

Little sisters here they come!
Under all this they really do care,
They're like a cuddly bear,
Little sisters here they . . . *come!*

Jack Kilbey (10)
Perryfields Junior School

Butterfly

Butterfly, oh butterfly,
Flying in the air.
Butterfly, oh butterfly,
Watching me brush my hair.

Oh what beautiful colours,
Red, white and gold,
Fit together nicely
And make you look so bold.

So much to say,
Who could describe this creature?
The fireman, the policeman,
Of course, not the teacher!

When Hallowe'en comes,
Are you frightened to death
And in some countries,
Do they keep you as a pet?

Oh so many,
Things about you I'd like to know
And have you ever heard or seen,
The incoming snow?

Maddison Cowie (10)
Perryfields Junior School

Puppy

My puppy is tiny, cuddly and cute,
He is sometimes naughty
And he runs off with my boot,
His fluffy tail wags all day,
He always wants me to play.
When he is awake he is mad,
Especially when he is bad,
He sleeps all day not long to play.

Samuel Taylor (8)
Perryfields Junior School

Autumn

The trees are changing
Before they look dead,
Vibrant green leaves
Turn to yellow and red.
Acorns and conkers fall to the ground,
Lying there waiting, soon to be found.
Soon the leaves will be gone,
The trees look so bare,
Branches like dead twigs
As if nothing had been there!
But now I know after a few months of waiting,
They're not dead, just hibernating!

Milly Drummond (10)
Perryfields Junior School

Autumn!

Leaves coming down in showers,
Leaves all red and gold,
Covering the little flowers
And tuck them in bed,
Spreading a fairy carpet,
Up the street
And when we skip along to school,
They rustle on our feet.

Tayla Johnson (10)
Perryfields Junior School

Saturday Morning

I'm playing football with my friend,
I score a goal at the end,
I'm doing flips and start to bend.

It's been raining and raining you should see the pitch,
Deary me it looks like a ditch,
I'm covered in mud I look like a witch.

I'm up and down on the field chasing the ball,
The ground is so wet I slip and I fall,
That means a trip to the hospital.

Joe Young (10)
Perryfields Junior School

Autumn Poem

Leaves turn red, orange, brown,
Leaves fall off the trees,
Blackberries ripen,
Then end up in pies for tea.

Children out hunting,
For the conkers, fallen off the trees,
Apples ripen,
Then end up in pies for tea.

Harvest is here,
Donate again,
Feed the people,
Make pies again.

Cameron Mear (10)
Perryfields Junior School

Flame Bird

Once I saw a bird flying in the sky
it was going past so quickly
I really wished that I could fly
around the deserts with this long-winged bird
which was faster than a car
squawk squawk as it shouted at me
flame bird flame bird came to me
the chocolate brown bird coming to me
I want to fly up with him but he is too quick
flame bird flame bird I will never be quick enough
to fly with you.

Jordan Magrath (8)
Perryfields Junior School

My Auntie's Dog

My auntie's dog is called Tinkerbell
She is muddy brown like a fuzz ball,
She is very crazy and wild,
Sometimes very hyper and also a bit funny,
She is very loud and fast but so cute,
She is pretty and soft but most of all fluffy!

Jasmin Hardwick-Box (8)
Perryfields Junior School

My Autumn Poem

A ll the leaves fall off the trees.
U nder the trees the squirrels hunt for acorns.
T he leaves are changing colour.
U nder the fallen leaves more and more conkers hide
M ixture of colours of red, yellow, orange and brown
N othing is more colourful than autumn.

Sam Templeman (11)
Perryfields Junior School

My Animal Poem

My dog is funny and very happy.
My dog likes to bark and he's got some patches.
My dog is sandy coloured and he's very sleepy.
My dog is fluffy and he's soft.
My dog is furry, he likes to jump up.
My dog is hairy and I love him.
My dog is called Patch.

Amy Jacobs (8)
Perryfields Junior School

Shoes!

Shoes are what I love to wear,
More than make-up or doing my hair,
Slip-ons, lace-ups, pink or white,
Heels so high they give you a fright.
Converse, No Fear and not forgetting Vans,
These are three of my favourite brands.
I wear them with skinny legs jeans,
This is what high fashion means.

Holly Raymond
Perryfields Junior School

My Autumn Poem

A utumn, my favourite season,
U nusual weather,
T ree leaves reds, golds and yellows,
U nder bonfires hedgehogs snuggle,
M y lucky conker,
N o one can beat it.

Alex Middlebrook (10)
Perryfields Junior School

Autumn Is . . .

Autumn is . . .
Gold, burgundy, red, ochre and yellow leaves falling from
                                     the stripped trees.
Crunchy crispy leaves scattered in the park, fallen off dying plants.
Glistening ripe berries ready to be picked by humans and birds alike.
Conkers ready for children to collect and battle with.
Squirrels rummaging around for acorns and nuts.
Ripe, juicy sweetcorn swaying in the breeze ready for harvesting.
Tall sunflowers bursting with seed waiting to be picked and kept for
                                     sowing the following year.
The Diwali festival of light is near and all the candles are being lit for
                                     the dark nights.
Hallowe'en is next with ghoulish bright orange pumpkins sitting on
           doorsteps and children wearing frightening costumes.
Bonfire Night follows soon with howling and deafening fireworks
                           shooting up into the pitch-black sky.
Autumn is one of the most exciting and fun seasons of the year.
Possibly because there is a special day in autumn that happens
                         every year and that day is my birthday.

Shailan Dhruv Gohil (11)
Perryfields Junior School

Rugby World Cup

I like to watch the Rugby World Cup
England had lots of luck.
I watched Scotland, Samoa and Argentina
Playing in a large arena.
I hope England wins as they are my favourite team
It would be my best ever dream.

Jack Williamson (10)
Perryfields Junior School

Ten Things Found In A Superhero's Pocket

A beaming grey laser Zapper which was stolen from the Kudlak
                                                    base in China,
A ghastly alien brain from Gallafrey,
An atomic time bomb which he found in Brazil in an encounter
                                                    with the Gorgons,
A superior fireball gun found on Pluto,
A jet pack that can go underwater,
Superhero chewing gum (half chewed),
A fake moustache and fake hair (disguise),
Fish food for his super fish Spyro,
A pencil and notebook to write things down,
Sonic hammer which can smash anything.

Joseph Williams (9)
Perryfields Junior School

Ten Things Found In A Superhero's Pocket

A cloak to make him invisible,
A parachute just in case he falls off a building,
A gun that shoots ice chunks,
A chewing gun packet that's really a laser,
A packet of superhero beans (they give you energy),
A jet pack (just in case he can't fly),
A very big pair of glasses,
A screwdriver that squirts fly spray,
A flying licence.

Lauren Shaw (9)
Perryfields Junior School

My Acrostic Hallowe'en Poem

H owling wind on a pitch-black night,
A ll the trick or treaters causing a fright.
L aughing and screaming everywhere,
L anterns swaying without a care.
O ver the moon up in the sky,
W itches are cackling as the night goes by.
E ngaging children in this pumpkin filled fun,
E ven apple bobbing and sweets that weigh a tonne!
N ow that's Hallowe'en . . . *mwa! Ha! ha! ha! ha!*

Mahlon King (10)
Perryfields Junior School

Autumn

A utumn is when the crispy leaves fall from the giant trees.
U gly yew trees start to grow multicoloured fungus.
T he time when the nights get shorter and darker.
U nderground, badgers and hedgehogs are hibernating.
M any birds fly south to a much warmer place.
N ever fear, winter is near!

Sam Thompson (10)
Perryfields Junior School

School

S chool is fantastic
C hildren playing with their friends
H aving fun with the equipment at playtime
O n Thursday school is nearly over for two days
O n Friday it's great because it's the end of the week
'L et's go home,' I say to my friends.

Amy Brewster (11)
Perryfields Junior School

Lost And Found

One day I woke up I did not feel a wet tongue on my face
And my dog was not playing with his lace in his usual place.
There were no muddy paw prints all over the floor
And he is usually scratching the door.
I went onto the computer and printed some posters out,
I went to different shops and asked them to stick them about.
Finally I got a call I knew he was not lost,
We took him home and he played in the compost.

Gemma Wilson (8)
Perryfields Junior School

My Poem

My dog likes to play ball
And he likes to crawl.
He's sweet but he's very neat.
He eats a lot and he's big as a pot.
He's got a small nose and tiny toes.
He goes *woof* and his tail goes *poof.*
He licks my feet and he doesn't like meat.

Georgia Robertson (8)
Perryfields Junior School

I Have A Dog

I have a dog who's loud,
He likes to turn around and be found.
I cuddle him and he smiles,
You could hear his bark from miles.
He's really cute and acts like a brute.
He's so, so crazy and he loves daisies.
He's really cool but he is a fool.

Paddy Wood (8)
Perryfields Junior School

Love!

Love is the colour of a bright red rose growing in the summer breeze.
Love smells like a drop of my favourite perfume.
Love sounds like 1 million hearts all beating at the same time.
Love is the shape of hundreds of butterflies soaring in the bright
blue sky.
Love looks like anything you have dreamt of.
Love makes you feel like you're worth 1 billion pounds.

Madeleine Bye (9)
Perryfields Junior School

Autumn Poem

Autumn time is here,
The leaves are changing colour.
Winter is near,
Autumn time is here.

The creatures start to sleep,
Loads of flowers die
Trees lose their leaves,
Autumn time is here.

People buy more coats,
No shorts or short sleeves,
Autumn time is here.
Sheep start to grow more wool,
Autumn time is here.

Swallows start to migrate,
Autumn time is here at last.

Calum Wilson (11)
Perryfields Junior School

The Tiger

If a tiger was playing and wanted to kill you
this is what he'd do,
pick up his paw and throw it at you,
watch out for the claw.
If a tiger was hungry and wanted to eat you
this is what he'd do,
open his jaw and charge at you,
watch out for the teeth.
A tiger may look like a household cat
but he can eat you, just like that.
If a tiger was scary and wanted to scare you
this is what he'd do,
open his powerful jaw and let out a mighty *roar!*

Sam Stuckey (8)
Perryfields Junior School

Lean, Mean, Killing Machine

I am mean, I am lean
I am the best killing machine.
I am very vicious,
My food is delicious,
Beware my sharp teeth
As I come from beneath.
I am grey, I am white
I fight with all my might.
Even though I'm so fast
You practically can't see me
As I go past.

Cameron Stevenson (8)
Perryfields Junior School

The Match

Sunday is here, the match is near
got to get on all my gear
number twelve is on my back
I'm in defence not in attack.
Team colours are red, white and blue
let's hope we score a goal or two.
Our goalkeeper is very good
he saves the goals just as he should.
Before the game we all warm up
We want to win that trophy cup!
The ref turns up, my nerves set in
Can we do it, can we win?
The whistle blows, so shout from the roof!
Give a cheer for Ravens Youth!

Aaron Green (7)
Perryfields Junior School

West Ham Beat Spurs

West Ham West Ham
Is all I can hear

West Ham West Ham
Booming in my ear

Come on you irons
The crowd start to sing

Come on your irons
Bellamy flies down the wing

We're forever blowing bubbles
Ashton scores a great goal

Three points to the Hammers
And the sack for Martin Jol.

Ashley Williams (10)
Perryfields Junior School

Fun

Fun is the colour of red,
Fun is the colour of blue,
Fun is the colour of green,
Fun is the colour of you.

Fun smells like me,
Fun smells like you,
Fun is really cool
Because you can play hide-and-seek and boo.

Fun sounds like laughing,
Fun sounds like cheering,
Fun sounds like playing,
Sometimes you can get really bad hearing.

Fun is the shape of a rainbow,
Fun is the shape of a slide,
Fun is the shape of a ball,
So you can shoot, miss and hide.

Fun looks like kicking,
Fun looks like running around,
Fun looks like shooting a ball
And laughing out loud.

Fun makes you feel happy,
Fun makes you feel cool,
Fun makes you feel gigantic
And really, really small.

Molly Reid (9)
Perryfields Junior School

Owls

Owls swooping and looping in the moonlight
Landing on trees and looking around in the night.
Owls eat anything but their favourite is mouse.
Some owls live in a nest, some in your house.

Robert White (8)
Perryfields Junior School

Fun

Fun is the colour of a rainbow in the sky.
Fun smells like chocolate, all melted into a yummy sauce.
Fun sounds like the world is obeying you and you are the ruler!
Fun is the shape of a huge adventure playground and not a
                                                        teacher in sight.
Fun looks like a cool person who has lots 'n' lots of friends.
Fun makes you feel like a gigantic pizza, but no one can eat you.

Shahzaib Shaikh (9)
Perryfields Junior School

Outdoors At Perryfields

Outdoors at Perryfields I see,
Leafy dark compost.

Outdoors at Perryfields I hear,
Howling invisible wind.

Outdoors at Perryfields I feel,
Sweet furry pollen.

Outdoors at Perryfields I smell,
Smoky smelly logs.

Gemma Longman (8)
Perryfields Junior School

Candles

C andles bright and shiny
A nd the wax runs down the side
N othing like a bright candle
D oes nothing but sits there and shines
L ife goes on but a candle just gets slim
E nd of the candle flickers and goes dim.

George Suttling (10)
Perryfields Junior School

Autumn

Here comes the browny orange leaves,
here comes the desolate trees that loom old and dead,
here comes the cooling breeze,
here comes the coats and gloves so wrap up warm,
here comes the dying flowers that are gone for another year like
        the lovely summer,
here comes the dark, cold mornings and the earlier, darker nights
        that come from autumn to winter,
here comes Christmas just around the corner so cheer up.

Karun Mistry (10)
Perryfields Junior School

Autumn

Leaves crunching under my feet,
Golden leaves glistening,
Spiderwebs shining in the limelight,
Frosty breezes blowing through,
Birds flying off to a warmer place and animals hibernating,
Hail falling from the sky, ouch, ouch, ouch,
Autumn is over now, winter's coming.

Campbell McLay-Kidd (9)
Perryfields Junior School

World War II

It's sad to be an evacuee to be sent away from home,
cardboard suitcase, box on a string,
Anderson shelter dug into the ground,
hidden by vegetables as bombs fall around,
With gas masks on, planes drop a bomb,
That's what happened to my great uncle John.

Megan Glover (7)
Perryfields Junior School

My Tortoises

My tortoise is called Tatiana,
She is very old,
She hibernates in the winter,
When it's very cold.

She has a baby called Anastasia,
She is nearly three,
We hatched her from an egg,
It was brilliant to see.

Their favourite food is dandelions,
They eat them every day,
On the floor of their hutches,
We put lots of hay.

People think tortoises are slow,
And they aren't very fast,
But mine go very quickly,
And in a race they wouldn't come last.

Adam Norton-Steele (8)
Perryfields Junior School

Puppy

Look at this puppy
He is cute and cuddly
Hear him bark
Because he's afraid of the dark
In the morning he is fast and furious
Wants to go for a walk because he is curious
When I feed him his eyes light up
This greedy puppy does not like muck.

Courtney Drury (8)
Perryfields Junior School

Fear

Fear is the colour of black, orange and gold,
Fear smells like oil and smoke,
Fear sounds like, 'Help! help!' and sounding sirens!
Fear is the shape of a car hurtling towards you at speed.
Fear looks like you're in a body bag.
Fear makes you feel dead,
Next thing you know you are.

Fear is black,
Fear is red,
Fear is blue,
Fear is gold.

Fear is flames inside your house burning,
Fear is everywhere,
Fear is making you scared,
Fear is nerves,
Fear needs guts!
And you need both to fight a fire if London's *burning!*

Jack Johnson (10)
Perryfields Junior School

Ten Things Found In A Magician's Hat

A very, very, very cute bunny,
A magic wand,
A bunch of flowers,
A magic potion,
Everlasting gobstoppers,
A potion book to show you how to make a cheese sandwich,
A book of spells,
A clown's flowers,
A spare hat
And a frog that can do cartwheels.

Georgia Bellsham (9)
Perryfields Junior School

Autumn Poem

Autumn is here
The leaves are crispy brown
Falling, tumbling to the ground
The cold is coming.

Some birds are off to migrate
Others come from different countries
All because
The cold is coming.

Animals are hibernating
Collecting food to store
Hedgehogs and squirrels too
The cold is coming.

Peter Gilbey (10)
Perryfields Junior School

My Flower Poem

Daffodils, crocuses
Snowdrops in the spring
Roses, carnations, the summer days bring
Autumn comes and the flowers will fade away
Here comes winter, no flowers or colour day after day.
Spring's here again.

Lauren Harris (10)
Perryfields Junior School

Chicken

Chicken all feathery pecking all day,
Comfy in the hen house laying on the hay.
They have a sharp beak to peck at the corn,
Sitting on eggs waiting for chicks to be born.

Artiom Evans (8)
Perryfields Junior School

My Dog Is Called Millie

My doggie is called Millie
She is mad as mad can be
We often think she's rather silly
She's also a best friend to me
She catches rabbits by their trails
But you know our dog only fails
So we shout out, 'Don't eat their tails!'

Leah Coggins (7)
Perryfields Junior School

Man Utd

M anchester United are the best
A lex Ferguson and all the rest
N o one can beat Man U

U nited just can't lose
T evez is a great striker
D ream team 2007!

Adam Jacobs (10)
Perryfields Junior School

Flowers

F lowers are pretty
L ovely as the sun
O n the ground they grow
W herever you look their colours are bright
E ven in the dark of the night
R oots start to spread in the morning light.

Jessica Carter (10)
Perryfields Junior School

My Dolphin Poem

The dolphins dive and jump all day
In the lovely sea
Then swim away
Quickly happy to be free.

The fast family of dolphins
Squeak and click all day
Under the surface of the sea
They love to dive and play.

They are blue and very hard to see
But glide fully in the sea,
I'd love to watch them swimming free,
But if you get close
They would probably flee.

Melissa Burton (8)
Perryfields Junior School

My Poem

Look at the dog,
He is scared of a frog,
But the frog
Isn't scared of the dog.
Look at the dog,
He's very soft,
But he doesn't like
To have a wash.
The dog is very nice,
But he doesn't like mice.
My dog doesn't like licking out of a bowl,
And he doesn't like digging a hole.
My dog loves running,
But he doesn't like coming.
My dog is very loud,
But he doesn't miaow
And I love my dog so much.

Lauren Clay (9)
Perryfields Junior School

Roses And Flowers

Roses smell in different ways
And look pretty in different ways
I smell and smell in the rosy days
I hope they last in the wintry days.

They shine in the beautiful hot sun
And glimmer and shimmer as the days pass on.

Flowers are different beautiful colours
Pink, yellow, red, blue and green
But some flowers are multicoloured
They shine and sway in the evening sun
Then close up once the night has begun
Until the morning comes again

Roses are the queen of flowers
But the other flowers are the pretty princesses
All the dresses are made with colourful petals
Oh I love my garden with all these beautiful flowers.

Alicia Thompson (7)
Perryfields Junior School

Football

F ootball is great fun.
O ffside is a foul in football.
O wen is the surname of a famous football player.
T he time in the whole game is 90 minutes
B eckham plays for England.
A t half-time everyone goes to get a hot dog.
L ong kicks are done by the goalkeeper.
L ucky shot 1-0!

Hannah Whiteley (10)
Perryfields Junior School

Poem Of A Guinea Pig

Soft, little kind guinea pig, adorable and brown.
Cuddle it, hold it, do lots of things around.
Sweet, cute, kind and furry, love it, love it, love all around.
Name is Dora, soft as a cat, small big,
Just the right size for you, Dora.

Dora you're very cute.
Dora you're very helpful and sweet.
Dora you love to sleep.
Dora you love to run, love to eat, love to dance and sing,
Love to do everything around.

Morgan Matthams (8)
Perryfields Junior School

Four-Legged Friends

He was here one minute ago now he's gone,
He's dead, he's in Heaven.
His footprints have faded on the lawn,
He's gone, he's dead.

He felt fluffy and soft when I stroked him.
He always barked soft and cutely.
He's gone, he's dead.

Sometimes when he had been rolling around in mud
He smelt a bit funny.
He's gone, he's dead.

Charlotte Perkins (8)
Perryfields Junior School

Football

The players come out
The whistles goes
Where will the ball go nobody knows
Yellow card, red card
In the last minute
A player breaks free
Strikes the ball firm and square
Straight past the keeper's hair
The crowd roars
One-nil to the home team
The whistle goes
The crowd cheers
What a game!

Samuel Tregaskes (9)
Perryfields Junior School

Elephant, Elephant

Elephant, elephant you're so big
With your long trunk reaching for that twig,
You love to dig and rummage for food,
But elephant, elephant you're in a mood!
Or is it that mouse that's scaring you so?
That's making you angry and your trunk blow!

Ben Gillyon (9)
Perryfields Junior School

The Rainbow

Soft, little kind guinea pig, adorable and brown,
The rainbow creeps over the sky.
Deposits from one side and arrives at another.
It looks over the world and hears peace.
Finally it fades away and goes to sleep.

Conor J Sherlock (10)
St Antony's RC Primary School, Woodford Green

My Washing Machine

There's a hole in my pants. It's our washing machine.
It's eating our clothes not washing them clean.
As it churns around and around it snorts and it snickers,
Chewing holes in Dad's shirts and ripping Mum's knickers.

It's swallowed a sock we can't open the door.
It's bubbling soap suds all over the floor,
There's a monster that lives in our washing machine,
It's eating our clothes not washing them clean.

Kelechi Ojiako (7)
St Antony's RC Primary School, Woodford Green

Rain

The rain spits angrily at the rocky, grey ground.
It hammers down on rooftops, soaking everything in its way.
It plants a miserable feeling, affecting the whole land.
It becomes tired and gets trapped in a white pillow,
Tucked up for the night.

Annabella King (11)
St Antony's RC Primary School, Woodford Green

School

As I walk into school I spot my strict teacher's face
As I walk into school she spots my undone lace
As I walk into school my friends pat me on the back
As I walk into school Mum gives me a smack
As I walk into school I say things to my friends
As I walk into school I see my classroom again
As I walk into school my teacher starts to yell
As I walk into school - got to go, there's the bell!

Charlotte Ring (9)
St Antony's RC Primary School, Woodford Green

Rage!

In a cage building your rage
Seeing faces of different races,
Hunting, killing it's all so thrilling,
Not looking through bars and smelling cars.

On your own all alone,
The future's frightening with no sign of brightening,
Seeing children all so small
And you're being treated so cruel.

Now you are free and left to be,
You are used to the wild,
Seeing nothing that's tiled,
A deer to the slaughter, there's a new daughter.

Killing prey in the hot weather of May,
It's all you thought it to be,
Living in the wild raising your child,
Without a cage there will be no rage.

Jordan Grace (10)
St Antony's RC Primary School, Woodford Green

Tree On The Pavement

A farmer buys me in a nursery
I feel like someone loves me

The farmer's friend plants me on a pavement
I can taste the water dripping on my feet and I grow

A dog walks past and I suddenly feel wet
I smell like a toilet

Teenagers draw on me
I feel scratched and sore

A woodcutter chops me down for paper
I feel abused and neglected.

Lydia Nugent (11)
St Antony's RC Primary School, Woodford Green

The Sun Is Setting

It's 9.25 on a midsummer's day and the sun is setting in
her own special way.
She is hiding behind the hills like a villager watching
as someone kills.
Soon her rays are popping out seeking a goodnight kiss.
The sunset is beautiful, it's pure bliss.

Francesca Hill (10)
St Antony's RC Primary School, Woodford Green

Tsunami

Rushing along in the bright blue sea,
feeling as powerful as ever.
A shape-shifter,
crashing into the shore.
Eating it up,
screams and shouts cry *tsunami!*
Then silence.

Olivia Gibson (10)
St Antony's RC Primary School, Woodford Green

Tornado

It danced upon the land,
Twisting and twirling,
Feeding on everything in its path,
Pushing back humans with its powerful arm,
Biting skin and pulling hair,
Screeching, screaming, shrieking shrilly;
It slowly backed away.

Louise Griffin (10)
St Antony's RC Primary School, Woodford Green

Sunset

She sits high in the blue sky
She is a ball of fire round and fiery
Her glowing light shines in the blue sky
At the end of the day she sinks into the atmosphere
And comes back tomorrow.

Niamh Fitzgerald (11)
St Antony's RC Primary School, Woodford Green

Life Losing Lightning

It picks things up like a pair of hands,
It whimpers like a tap turning on and off,
It smells like burning firewood,
The eyes are like flashing light bulbs,
Its colour is like bright neon,
And some people think that it will not stop,
Then all of a sudden it stops,
People say to them, 'Will it come back?'

Melissa Foakes (10)
St Teresa's RC Primary School, Basildon

The Sun

The sun is hot
The sun can burn

The sun is hot
The sun comes out

The sun is hot
The sun goes down.

Tony Stewart (10)
St Teresa's RC Primary School, Basildon

Hurricane Dean

Hurricane Dean a fast athlete,
Roaring like a fearsome lion,
The angry eye looking at the thick darkness,
The flat nose smelling land,
Dangerous as a shark,
It is a raging bull,
Hurricane Dean remembered.

Shelby Jarrett-Fenton (10)
St Teresa's RC Primary School, Basildon

The Crackling Of the Ice!

My skin was breaking from the weight above,
I screamed in silence,
As my back was broken,
My nerve endings tingled in fear,
The heavy boots walking on top of me,
Like drums pounding in my head,
I need the sun to come out,
So it will melt away my pains.

Vicky Oshunremi (11)
St Teresa's RC Primary School, Basildon

Waves

The move is super quick and raging
The sound is splashing and crashing
The smell is salty and cold
The smile is as high as a lighthouse
And most of all it is as mad as Davey Jones.

Devon Sloley (10)
St Teresa's RC Primary School, Basildon

Snow

As the snow fell the world got covered by a soft blanket
as white as glistening talc powder on a baby's back.

Then as the snowflakes dropped out of the cold sky
they were like small balls of cold cotton wool.

The snow whispered to the world friendly
as if they knew each other.

As more and more snowflakes fell
each flake after flake cuddled the clouds.

As midday came the flakes laid calmly on the floor.
There was a crunch every time one fell.

Pitter-patter, pitter-patter the snow was melting
and the snowflakes turned into a big puddle on the floor.

As the sun fell and the moon came up
and the snowflakes said goodnight.

Georgia Anderson (10)
St Teresa's RC Primary School, Basildon

Whimpering Wind

The spoilt wind moans and whimpers for attention.
It bullies the trees throwing punches to beat the branches.

It sulks and strops to get its own way,
The temper tantrums last for days or minutes giving up the fight.

Like a hungry lion it stays on its prey.

The wind is never going to grow up.

Deborah Shobande (10)
St Teresa's RC Primary School, Basildon

Sunset

It awakens behind the horizon.
It is red wool.
The water sways and the sun smiles.
The clouds cuddle the sun.

Its face smiling at the Earth.
Play and seek behind the clouds.
The sun reflects on the ice rink water.
As it giggles then disappears.
Ice skaters on the water dancing all night long.

The orange sunset fades every day; again and again.
The sun falls then rises and people watch the sunset.

The sun disappears behind the horizon until tomorrow!

Zainab Williams (10)
St Teresa's RC Primary School, Basildon

Water Storm

W ind in a twister,
A loud and long drum roll,
T ipping water from a boiled kettle,
E verlasting smashing glass,
R aging sea.

S tanding person rolling over,
T urning twister,
O n a watery bed,
R unning fast on slippery ice on the bumpy floor.
M isty water on a dark sea like a melting ice cube.

Jack Anderson (10)
St Teresa's RC Primary School, Basildon

Snow!

He leaps across the mountains
Ballet dances across the sugar coated grass,
He lies upon a fountain,
His slippers form footprints in the snow.

He sits upon a cloud scattering snow from his hands.
Taking notice of the level,
As he peers across the lands,
His dancers leap from tree to tree.

Soft as a million mattresses laid upon the floor,
He sprinkles and he sprinkles,
Until he can sprinkle no more,
He gently floats down to the ground.

He waits around until dawn comes,
Because he will melt,
By the heat of the sun,
He says goodbye.

Ellie Nugent (10)
St Teresa's RC Primary School, Basildon

Snow

The snow goes face flat on the ground,
Then turns into layers to keep us warm.

Its eyes are little and shining,
When they fall it is like sky diving out the clouds.

Gently lying round the tree like ballerinas dancing around the tree.
When it falls it falls like cotton wool in your hand.

Judith Mason (10)
St Teresa's RC Primary School, Basildon

This Thing In The Sky As Fast As Light

This thing in the sky as fast as light,
Comes in your bedroom in the night,
Every night he holds you tight.

No one knows where he goes,
I'm pretty sure he has big bows,
His head smells like silly toes.

In his crystal marble he has a ball,
That has powers to grow really tall,
Everyone knows that it's cool,
So every night look up into the sky
And dream!
Of . . .
Lightning!

Fleur Campbell (10)
St Teresa's RC Primary School, Basildon

The Waves

Waves are smooth and soft
Wish, wish, wish
Splash, splash, splash
Relaxing water that cools you down

Going up and going down
Swish, swish, swish

The blue waves to do surfing, swimming,
Lots of things you can do.
It simply wouldn't be life
Without the waves.

Matthew Spooner (10)
St Teresa's RC Primary School, Basildon

Terror Tornado

It dances around and around until it stops,
Time flies by upon the clock.
People run for their lives,
Children and babies cry,
But in the eyes there are loads of flies.
As the twister goes on bits and bobs fly by.
It moves closer and closer it whistles a tune like a man,
Jingling noises for pans.
Things come rushing,
Cars are crushing.
People running,
Parents cunning.
And . . .
It smells like old pans,
It moves around like a big clown.
It goes and goes,
Then it flows.
But people know it's a big dancer spinning.

Hollie Magner (10)
St Teresa's RC Primary School, Basildon

Freaky Thunder

Banging drums as the rain pours down.
Loud as elephants stomping the ground.
Sneaky jump on people when not expecting.
Sounds like an explosion never-ending.
As the rain pours,
Sounds like snores.
Where everyone is trying to get to bed.
The noise is loud enough to wake the dead!

Michael Tucker (10)
St Teresa's RC Primary School, Basildon

I Am A Waterfall

I am scary
   I am funny
      I am bossy
         I am greedy
            I am gross
               I am ugly
                  I am sad
                     I am 2,000 foot high
                             I am never known
                               I am never seen.

John Sagomba (10)
St Teresa's RC Primary School, Basildon

The World Wave

The world was watching the waves on the beach
Then everyone heard a little girl screech.
She said to everyone with bumps on her arms,
'A wave is coming so be alarmed.'
As they looked back they saw it coming,
So they started running.
The wave was faster and they all had to use
At least one hundred plasters.
After a year or two they came back and said,
'Let's hope it doesn't happen to you.'

Ellen Smith (10)
St Teresa's RC Primary School, Basildon

Snow

Snow crackles like it is laughing.
Snow crackles like it bubbles in a bath.
Snow crackles under your feet.

Snow walks like you and me.
Snow walks under your shoes.
Snow walks when it is on your clothes.

Snow flies on the tree.
Snow flies like clouds of sugar.
Snow flies like a sky diver.

Snow is like Plasticine you can mould.
Snow is like mountains of candyfloss.

Angel Hart (10)
St Teresa's RC Primary School, Basildon

The Storm

It moves like a running tap
It is as noisy as a Year 6 classroom.

It smells like salt
It has eyes of God.

As fast as a cheetah
As high as a block of flats.

The storm is as big as a bubble bath.

Mitch Langley (11)
St Teresa's RC Primary School, Basildon

Fire

Fire starts on a hot day,
It finds its way
To every beautiful thing in sight,

The fire rips everything until they are too damaged
To be beautiful again to brighten up the world,

The fire sounds like a sparkler being lit up
Over and over again but it is getting louder each and every time,

All of the things shiver and die and the fire carries on until
It is too tired to go on,

Then suddenly stops and the fire has gone,
All that is left is the sparkles lighting up the night.

Brogan Morgan (10)
St Teresa's RC Primary School, Basildon

Sun!

The sun is a giant eye, staring at the sea making it shimmer
                                                    in its light.
The sun runs across the sky getting hotter and hotter.
The air shimmers as the sun dances in the light blue sky.
The sun beams on the giant waves as they splash on the sea.
The day comes to an end and the sun slips away.

Sam Murray (10)
St Teresa's RC Primary School, Basildon

Silence!

Silence can hurt you wherever you are,
It tips red wine all over your dress.
Silence can hurt you in your car,
Nothing can make it hurt you less.

Silence is the sound you have never heard,
It haunts you wherever you go.
Silence doesn't let you hear the sound of the bird,
It's the sound you'll never know.

Silence is the image of the shadow,
It is with you all the time.
Silence is the saying oh no!
It takes away your winning dime.

Silence will follow you now and then,
It says words that will scare you.
Silence follows me and I'm only ten,
It might follow you too!

Alice Davidson (10)
Wells Primary School

Darkness

Darkness is like the moon shining on the rushing sea.
Darkness sounds like footsteps outside your bedroom door.
Darkness tastes like bitter, hot, burnt toast with a horrid taste.
Darkness smells like thick, black smoke whirling all around.
Darkness is black like the night air when you're in bed.
Darkness feels like the icy wind pushing against my face.

Christy Gilbert (8)
Wells Primary School

The Bird

A bird sitting in a tree,
Jumped around and winked at me
She sang a song as if to say
Hello how are you today.

The bird red and white
Had a big fright
She saw a bird next to me
Which had just come from the tree.

He sang to the bird
You must go away I heard
The bird flew high
Up, up in the sky.

I started to walk
Birdy started to talk
We both sat down
But we didn't frown.

I took him home
But he went away to a dome
I really miss him
For evermore my life is dim.

Abigail Saffron (10)
Wells Primary School

Rugby

R ugby is rough and tough
U nion rugby is the best
G reat passing and drop kicks
B leeding faces and big scars
Y ards from the try line snatching the ball.

Joseph Morgan (11)
Wells Primary School

The Dragon

What a shout
The dragon is back
This time there's no doubt!

He burns you like Grandma's Sunday roast
Unfortunately it was no idle boast.

He is in a tower
But when he breaks
There's no knight on this Earth that wouldn't cower.

He's like the dragon of steel
But never go close
Then you will be his meal.

He waits till you're in his sight
What a fright!

Never mistake him for a friend
Foe's the word
Or you will meet your end!

A drop of tears may appear
But never show any fear
Because he wouldn't care.

His fire never tires
His wings never collapse
And his feet are always ready to do another 100 laps.

No crying, no dragon has emotions,
Except for a wicked grin
When he takes you in

Beware of the dragon
It's no holiday being in its presence
And when it gets tense
Oh! sorry
I need to go to the gents.

Joe Philpott (9)
Wells Primary School

Fluttering Here All Year

Fluttering in the garden all year round,
Here are the flowers I have found.
Pinks and yellows during spring,
From the daffodils and tulips which form a ring.

As these flowers witter and fall,
The cherry blossoms brighten it all.
Summer comes with longer days,
As the sun extends its rays.

The gentle scent that lavender brings,
High above the apple tree the beautiful birds sing.
Days are short nights are long,
Winters are full of Christmas songs.

Poppies in November,
Hollies in December,
Making this a real year to remember.

Geraldine Wan (9)
Wells Primary School

Fun Is . . .

Making your own pizza
and then sharing it with your cousins

Taking old bread and rolls
and feeding it to the ducks on the river

Watching a dog come out of the water
and then shake himself dry all over everyone

Hiding in the wood and bushes
then jumping out to scare your parents
Boo!

Elizabeth Stoney (7)
Wells Primary School

Dinosaurs

Dinosaurs are big and strong,
Dinosaurs, they lived for so long.

Dinosaurs, some fat, some tall,
Dinosaurs, some thin, some small.

Dinosaurs, some nice, some scary,
Dinosaurs, some plain, some hairy.

Dinosaurs, they love to eat,
Dinosaurs, some love meat.

Dinosaurs are admired by us,
Dinosaurs are longer than a bus.

Dinosaurs, some have spikes,
Dinosaurs, they make us shout, 'Yikes!'

Dinosaurs, they make us think
Dinosaurs, they've become extinct.

Joshua Fernandez-Steele (10)
Wells Primary School

The Dressmaker Of York

The dressmaker of York
Fancied some pork,
So she went to Germany,
But there wasn't any,
So she came back,
At the airport she lifted off a sack,
Which held all her things,
She was back in a puff,
It was the night,
But her sack was light,
She went home,
Where she was all alone
And bought some from the corner shop,
'What a waste! The pork's a paste! I better find some again!'

Sarah Zheng (9)
Wells Primary School

Autumn Days

Harvest time has been and gone,
All the fields are looking dull.
Mushrooms pop up their heads,
And mornings have a misty start.

Conkers dropping on people's heads,
Soon they will be done and dusted.
Some leaves on the trees are turning brown,
While others are starting to fall.

Winter clothes are nearly out to play,
Walking to school is getting so chilly.
Brown and orange replaces green.
Squirrels collect their acorns ready for winter.

A whistle through the trees.
The sound of rain on the windowpane.
I wish this scene would never end.
Next year it is sure to be the same.

Lydia Watkins (9)
Wells Primary School

Changes

I'm alone in the dark, and in a bit of a spin,
But I'm stuck to the ground with a sharp-ended pin.
I'm wriggling out, but my head keeps twirling,
I have no torch and the birds aren't chirping.

But I'm back in the light; my head's not spinning,
And back in the distance I can hear people singing.
Now I'm not alone, there are people around me
And now everybody is starting to crowd me.

I am happy here because the birds are chirping
And because of the background my head isn't twirling . . .

Annie Cowen (7)
Wells Primary School

My Family

My sister

My sister has tanned skin and black hair,
for a big girl she has a big teddy bear.
People say we look alike,
especially when we are riding our bikes.
Her birthday is on the 17th of March,
most of the time we would visit the arch.
She likes to watch 'Buffy',
but when it doesn't play she gets puffy.
She likes to clean
but if we make a mess she gets mean.

My mum

My mum cooks really nice food,
it always puts me in a good mood.
She is very caring,
especially when I have been good and sharing.

My parrot Raju

Raju has different names,
he always likes to play games.
He is very active
and his feathers are very attractive.
He is grey and has a red tail,
Raju is a male.

My dad

My dad loves me a lot,
he takes me out when the weather is hot.
He likes to watch football,
we can hear him cheering down the hall.

Divya Ramesh Arjan (7)
Wells Primary School

Winter

Winter come as autumn fades
Icy cold wind pricks my face.

Winter woollies in the shops
My pink puffer jacket and my long warm socks.

It grows colder as it grows darker
It's time for my dad to wear his parka.

My mum starts moaning as the rain pours down
As my grin soon changes to a frown.

When I come home my cheeks are rosy red
I can't wait to snuggle up in bed.

The icy cold snow falls heavily down and down
It's already covered half of the town.

Snowball fights in the all-white park
We fire away until dark.

Christmas is coming I can't wait
For all those presents and turkey on my plate.

Winter's wet, cold and windy but really it's not so bad
Because Christmas comes, it's festive season
So I'm glad winter comes, I'm glad!

Eleanor Richardson (9)
Wells Primary School

Darkness

Darkness is as black as ink, rushing out the tip of the pen.
Darkness sounds like the monster under the bed,
Darkness smells like a damp night, wet with moss,
Darkness looks like nothing, nothing, nothing there,
Darkness tastes like a witch's brew,
Darkness feels like spiders crawling everywhere,
All over your body as you get buried under the soil.
Darkness reminds me of my death.

Mia Berelson (10)
Wells Primary School

Seasons

When I think of spring I think of newborn animals
such as lambs, birds, chicks and bunnies
summer flowers blooming

When I think of summer I think of hot, lazy afternoons,
ice creams, yellow beaches.

I think of suntan lotion, games in the sand,
Splashing waves and people seated in the sun
like pink fish.

When I think of autumn it means to me
playing in leaf piles on cold misty mornings,
collecting conkers, going to bonfires
and smelling the smoke in the evening air
standing on the squidgy soil
and coming home waiting for tomorrow

Autumn means to me cuddling my teddy
and sitting watching the sun slowly fade away
and the fireworks starting

When I think of winter I think of Santa's elves
hot cocoa, presents, snowmen, frost, snow, Rudolph, reindeers
And I long to see the sun again.

Georgia Roberts (8)
Wells Primary School

Fireworks!

F ireworks exploding
I n the ink black sky
R eleasing millions of shooting stars
E verywhere lit with the colours of the rainbow
W ide-eyed children staring into the blackness
O nly the sound of
R ockets whistling into the still air a
K aleidoscope of sound and colour and then all
S ilent, oh how I love fireworks night.

Laura Harvey (7)
Wells Primary School

Animals In The Darkness

Animals scratch, animals scare
Animals jump out everywhere.

Tooting owls and whining cats
Flapping nervously tip tap bats.

Foxes jump and foxes play
In amongst the farmer's hay.

Hedgehogs run and hedgehogs scurry
Looking for food in a hurry.

We must respect our friends of the forest,
Keep our woods and never demolish.

Jessica Scott (7)
Wells Primary School

My Mum!

My mum's the best
better than the rest

Everyone thinks I'm mad
because I think her better than my dad

She helps me when I've got a really hard test
and loves to read her digest

She takes me out
without me having to shout

She is really fun
and likes to put her hair in a bun

She likes to go to the gym
and she likes to win

She's very sporty
and never faulty

So that's my mum, she's the *best!*

Noor Jamal (11)
Wells Primary School

Nonsense

'Walk a little faster will you, I haven't got all day!'
Said a little snail, who was making his own way.

'Where shall we go?'
'Somewhere just right!'
'Ooh, New York looks good!'
'OK, when's the flight?'

They both trailed along and
Two years later, found an airport,
'Aren't we two years overdue?'
'Don't worry, we'll just . . .' *Squash!*

Poor little snails,
They didn't live long,
They still don't understand,
What they did wrong!

Kitty Mae Atkins (10)
Wells Primary School

My Space

We're running out of space,
We're running out of time,
Do something *now!*
Because this world is yours and *mine!*

Chugging cars with corrupt exhausts,
The glimmer of glass flashing in the street,
A man drops a sweet wrapper which now tastes bitter,
Why should it be in our air and under our feet!

The ice is melting, the trees cut down,
The world and animals screaming,
'Help me now!'
But the man is making a big fat buck,
So it's not a major problem, it's just tough luck.

Lillian Delves (9)
Wells Primary School

The Seasons

From autumn,
To summer,
To winter,
To spring.

In Earth it's just a natural thing.
In winter it is cold,
In summer it is hot,
In spring . . .
I don't know,
I just forgot!

In autumn,
All the leaves fall off trees,
Now I remember,
In spring there is a light breeze.

In summer it is quite hot,
And with all the activities,
I get quite a lot!

In spring it's a bit boring,
I could stay in my room snoring!

In autumn it's beautiful,
I can't stop looking everywhere on the way to school!
My favourite season is winter because I like a snowball fight
And if I were allowed I'd play all *night!*

Atif Siddiqui (10)
Wells Primary School

Witch At Night

A dark witch, jet-black
gliding through the moonlit night,
cloak flying behind her.

Inky, sinful cat
clawing on the broomstick,
eyes bright against the starry night.

The witch flies swiftly,
wind whistling past her ears
rushing through the raging storm.

Where will her journey end?
Will it be
with her friends
at a Hallowe'en party
with their cauldrons bubbling?

Or does she travel
back home to
a glorious fire
with tea and cookies . . .

Louise Ranken (10)
Wells Primary School

Young Writers Information

We hope you have enjoyed reading this book - and that you will continue to enjoy it in the coming years.

If you like reading and writing poetry drop us a line, or give us a call, and we'll send you a free information pack.

Alternatively if you would like to order further copies of this book or any of our other titles, then please give us a call or log onto our website at www.youngwriters.co.uk

**Young Writers Information
Remus House
Coltsfoot Drive
Peterborough
PE2 9JX**

(01733) 890066